THE COMPLETE GUIDE TO
CLIMBING
(BY BIKE)

A guide to cycling climbing and the most
difficult hill climbs in the United States

John Summerson

Extreme Press
405 Kettle Court
Winston-Salem, NC 27104
336 659-7600
Extreme.press@yahoo.com

Library of Congress Card Number 2007900654

ISBN 13: 978-0-9792571-0-0
ISBN 10: 0-9792571-0-7

Front cover - Onion Valley Road in the eastern Sierras

Back cover - The road to Tioga Pass in California

Distributors:

Individual orders can be filled through Amazon.com and other online retailers or at extreme.press@yahoo.com

Book stores should contact Brigham Distribution at brigdist@sisna.com or 435 723-6611

Bike shops should contact American Cycling Inc at 800 282-2453

*"The best climbers do not suffer less;
they just suffer faster"* - Chris Boardman

Table of Contents

Preface/Acknowledgments 8
Introduction 9
    Climbing 9
    About this Guidebook 10
        Defining a hill climb. 11
        Definitions of Terms 12
        Rules of the Road 14
Improving Climbing Ability 15
    Cycling Techniques 15
    Specific Training for Hill Climbing 15
    Descending 19
    Mental Training 19
    Climbing Tactics 20
Memorable Climbing Performances. 22
Map Legend 32
Map of Climbs 33

NORTHEAST

Massachusetts
1. Mount Greylock (north). 34
2. Kingsley Hill Road 34

New Hampshire
3. Mount Washington** 36

New York
4. Whiteface Mountain* 38

Vermont
5. Lincoln Gap 40
6. Burke Mountain*. 40
7. Mount Auscutney* 42
8. Okemo Mountain*. 42
9. Mount Equinox* 42

SOUTHEAST

Georgia
10. Brasstown Bald*. 44

North Carolina
11. 19/Waterrock Knob 46
12. Cherohala Skyway (east) 46

13. Clingmans Dome (west)* 46
14. Beech Mountain 48
15. Roan Mountain (north)* 48
16. Mount Mitchell* 48

WEST

Arizona

17. Mincus Mountain (east) 50
18. Humboldt Mountain 50
19. Mount Graham* 52
20. Mount Lemmon* 52
21. Kitt Peak* 52

California

22. Mount Shasta* 54
23. Lassen National Park (south) 54
24. Monitor Pass (east)* 56
25. Monitor Pass (west) 56
26. Sonora Pass (west)* 56
27. Sonora Pass (east) 58
28. Tioga Pass (east) 58
29. Rock Creek Road* 58
30. Pine Creek Road* 60
31. Lake Sabrina* 60
32. South Lake* 60
33. Glacier Lodge Road* 62
34. White Mountain** 62
35. Death Valley Road (east)* 64
36. Death Valley Road (west) 64
37. Onion Valley Road** 66
38. Whitney Portal** 66
39. Horseshoe Meadows** 68
40. Nine Mile Grade* 68
41. Wildrose* 70
42. Emigrant Pass (east)* 70
43. Emigrant Pass (west)* 70
44. Townes Pass (east)* 72
45. Townes Pass (west)* 72
46. Daylight Pass* 74
47. Daylight Pass Long* 74
48. Dantes View* 74
49. Old Priest Grade 76

50. Cold Springs Summit* 76
51. Tollhouse Road/168* 78
52. 168* 78
53. 180* 80
54. Kings Canyon* 80
55. J21/245/180* 80
56. 245/180* 82
57. Sequoia* 82
58. Mineral King Road* 82
59. 190* 84
60. Parker Pass (west) 84
61. Shirley Meadows (east)* 84
62. Shirley Meadows (west) * 86
63. Sherman Pass (west)** 86
64. S22 88
65. Palomar Mountain* 88
66. 74 (east) 88
67. Valley of the Falls Road* 90
68. Angeles Oaks 90
69. 330* 90
70. 18 (south)* 92
71. 18 (north)* 92
72. N4/Table Mountain* 94
73. N4/Blue Ridge Summit* 94
74. 138/Lone Pine Canyon/Table Mountain* 94
75. 138/Lone Pine Canyon/Blue Ridge Summit* 96
76. Mount Baldy* 96
77. 39* 98
78. 39/Crystal Lake* 98
79. Mount Wilson 98
80. Fargo Street 100
81. Eldred Street. 100
82. Baxter Street 100
83. Mount Pinos 102
84. San Marcos/Painted Cave Road* 102
85. Gibraltor Road* 102
86. Figueroa Mountain Road (east)* 104
87. Figueroa Mountain Road (west) 104
88. Nacimiento Fergusson Road (west) 106
89. Bohlman/On Orbit 106
90. Bohlman Road 106

91. Alba Road* 108
92. Hicks/Mount Umunhum* 108
93. Marin Avenue 108

Colorado
94. Trail Ridge (east)* 120
95. Mount Evans** 120
96. Juniper Pass (west) 122
97. Loveland Pass (south) 122
98. Independence Pass (west)* 122
99. Pikes Peak 124
100. Cottonwood Pass* 124
101. Monarch Pass (west) 124
102. Slumgullion Pass (west) 126
103. Red Mountain Pass (north) 126
104. East Portal* 126
105. Grand Mesa (north)* 128
106. Grand Mesa (south)* 128
107. Colorado National Monument (east) 128

Hawaii
108. Haleakala** 130
109. Baldwin/Olinda Road* 130
110. Mauna Kea** 132
111. Mauna Loa** 132
112. Stainback Road* 132

Nevada
113. Rose Summit (north)* 134
114. Wheeler Peak* 134
115. Mount Charleston* 136
116. 157/158* 136
117. 156* 138
118. 156/158* 138

New Mexico
119. Sandia Crest* 140
120. Cloudcroft* 140

Oregon
121. Mount Hood* 142
122. Bear Camp Summit (west)* 142
123. Mount Ashland* 142

Utah

124. Guardsman Pass (west)* 144
125. Little Cottonwood Canyon* 144
126. Alpine Summit (east) 144
127. Nebo Loop Road (north) 146
128. 31 (west)* 146
129. Castle Valley 146
130. 153/Elk Meadows* 148
131. 153 148
132. 143 (north)* 148
133. Cedar Canyon 150
134. Right Hand Canyon 150
135. Kolob Reservoir Road* 150

Washington

136. Hurricane Ridge* 152
137. Mount Spokane* 152

Wyoming

138. Powder River Pass (west)* 154
139. Granite Pass (west)* 154
140. 14 (east)* 156
141. Alternate 14* 156
142. Teton Pass (east) 158
143. Beartooth Pass (east) 158
144. Snowy Range Pass (east) 158

Hill Climb Races 160
Organized Rides with Significant Climbing 162
Most Difficult Climbs 163
Most Difficult Climbing Sections 165
Greatest Elevation Gain Climbs 166
Highest Elevation Attained Climbs 167
Steepest Climbs/Fastest Descents/Most Scenic Climbs 168
Major Tour King of the Mountains/U.S. Hillclimb Race Winners 169
Climbing Resources 173
Climb Profiles 175

* Top 100 most difficult climb

** Top 10 most difficult climb

Preface

I believe my interest in climbing big hills began in July of 1982 in Tucson, Arizona. Trying to escape the scorching summer desert heat a friend and I were driving up massive Mt. Lemmon just north of town. Mt. Lemmon, called an island mountain and which are somewhat common in the southwest U.S., rises to over 9,000 feet almost straight up from the flat desert plain and the road to its top gains more than 6,000 feet in elevation. Heading up the mountain we passed a lone cyclist struggling up the hill. Sweating profusely in the mid day sun he had already covered many miles and over 3,000 vertical feet and was still only halfway to the top. I know I will always remember my reaction to that sight. Always physically active, I had recently purchased my second road bike, using it for occasional hard rides and to get back and forth from college classes. But I was not sure I could have made that climb. Our reaction was immediate and one of awe and respect. This rider was taking on a very difficult physical challenge. Once at the very top we had an even greater appreciation of his feat. From that day forward I have had an admiration for big hills and what it takes to climb them by bike.

I eventually rode Mt. Lemmon and it was soon evident that I wanted to find others to climb. While a few U.S. climbs were well known, there was no resource available that contained this information so I was left to stumble onto big hills, occasionally getting a piece of local information that panned out or discovering many simply by checking maps and then exploring. Time passed and I was able to live in several areas that contained significant climbing. Due to my interests and profession I was also able to travel quite extensively within the more mountainous regions of the country which eventually led to the location of America's most difficult hill climbs.

While being able to experience big hills certainly brings about a reaction, the super hills bring about something more. Just standing on Mount Washington's slopes in New Hampshire, which may be the toughest climb on earth, generates a sense of excitement and a bit of fear as you anticipate its difficulties. Haleakala in Hawaii is so long that it is hard to imagine getting to the top but the views of the Pacific Ocean help lead the way and you find that with some preparation it can be done. Marin Avenue in Berkeley, California, has one of the most difficult stretches of climbing anywhere as you must brave traffic, several stop signs, and extended 25% grade along the way. Standing at the bottom looking up toward its top is quite intimidating. Many other hills are out there and will make you wonder, can I make it? Today I still get a sense of satisfaction from finding another particularly challenging hill to climb.

Acknowledgments

There are many people that contributed to the creation of this guidebook. The most helpful include Jim Ainsley and Roy Ellefsen, whose knowledge of European climbs is quite amazing (next project), and the hill climb nuts on the KOMcycling usegroup, most notably Steven Sweedler and Frank Obusek. Others include the fine folks at Paceline Bike Shop, Robert Swickley, Brian Shilling and Shawn O'Malley out in Wyoming, Kevin Bullock, and Michael Kelsey, whose broad knowledge of guidebook publishing was of great help.

Introduction

Road bike cycling is one of the most popular sports in the world and the biggest challenge within the sport, and its most intriguing aspect, is hill climbing. Major professional cycling tours such as the Tour de France are usually won and lost in the mountains. But why climb the hill? Climbing is also the most difficult part of cycling, requiring great energy and effort and on tough hills or going all out, producing pain. Why, then, do cyclists routinely engage in a painful activity that can result, as they themselves describe, in great suffering for the sole purpose of reaching the top? In the case of professional riders it could be argued that they are paid to do it. For others answers may include losing weight, improving one's racing ability or fitness level, or getting back to where you started. But I think the real answer is because it's there. This simple phrase sums up the main reason people undertake physical challenges. Be it mountain climbing, distance running or peak-bagging by bike, the main reason cyclists will tolerate the pain is for the physical and mental challenge itself. Hills are there to be beaten.

For years, major cycling events such as the Tour de France have evoked the image of the lone rider struggling up sheer alpine pitches, straining their physical limits. Cycling greats such as Eddy Merckx, Bernard Hinault and Lance Armstrong, while very complete all-around riders, became legends in the sport in large part from their climbing exploits. The mountains add an almost mythic quality to races as the riders are seen overcoming obstacles that extend beyond the actual asphalt, rock and dirt upon which they climb. Even average cyclists feel the allure of attempting difficult climbs and achieve tremendous satisfaction from a successful summit. It sounds pretty simple. Find a mountain with a paved road to the top and then pedal up it. However, hill climbing is not easy, as certain climbs involve ascents of thousands of vertical feet. Elite riders can race to the top but success for most involves just getting there.

With a major portion of the country being mountainous, the United States has, while relatively unknown, many challenging hills to conquer; from the short and not-so-sweet 35% grade of Canton Avenue in Pittsburgh, Pennsylvania to the thirty-five-plus mile continuous-climb grinders of Hawaii. This book is meant to be a resource for road bike hill climbing and also describes the most difficult climbs in the U.S. Other climbs are included for reasons such as a steep grade, high altitude attained or other unique aspects.

Climbing

No one may know when the first significant hill was climbed on a bicycle but the first documentation of major ascents occurred in stage races which originated in Europe, the oldest being the Tour de France. It is interesting to note that the first two Tours (first held in 1903) did not include any mountain passes. Bikes were heavy, single speed (and brake) behemoths while many roads were unpaved. Some felt that the riders of the day could not complete big climbs and that adding them to the race route would ruin the Tour. It was not until 1905 that significant climbs were added, the very first being the Ballon d'Alsace in the Vosges Mountains. In 1910 the first major, high altitude passes were added (four major climbs in the Pyrenees Mountains including the now famous Tourmalet) which resulted in a great deal of criticism directed at race organizers that the routes were too difficult. As is often the case human potential was underestimated as many riders of that era conquered the climbs in dramatic fashion. In contrast, 1910 was also the year that the broom wagon was introduced to sweep riders up who could not finish the stage. In 1911 the first major climb in the Alps was added (Col de Galibier) with spectacular results. Instead of being a detriment, the uphill duels captured the public imagination and added to the popularity of the event. The race route every year thereafter has contained many significant climbs. Other major tours that followed also began to include hills along their routes. In 1933 the Tour de France and the Giro d'Italia (Italy's national tour) began recognizing the best climbers in the field (Spain's Vicente Trueba was the first winner in the Tour along with Alfredo Binda in the Giro). Most of the major stage races now recognize this accomplishment as the cyclists earn points based upon their finish in a climb and its difficulty. The cyclist with the most accumulated points is awarded the Polka Dot Jersey as the winner of the king of the mountains competition.

The performances of great early climbers such as Alfredo Binda, Fausto Coppi and Charley Gaul continued to increase the popularity of the major tours. These events made climbs such as the Tourmalet and L'Alpe d'Huez in France and Stelvio in Italy as well known to cycling fans as the Daytona Speedway or Yankee Stadium are to U.S. racing and baseball fans respectively. The mountains allowed bike races to become truly great as the event rose beyond the personal concerns of the cyclists to reflect life as a whole. Today hill climbing is more popular than ever and within multi-stage races those with hilltop finishes are usually the most anticipated and best attended stages of the race. Racing fans know that hills offer the best opportunity to view the drama within the peloton as it struggles through the most difficult and important element in any race. Climbing adds the mythic quality of overcoming obstacles that continues to be associated with the major cycling tours and which has produced many memorable moments. Ascending difficult hills is about struggle and perseverance and it is these aspects that have made conquering the mountains the heart and soul of cycling.

About This Guidebook

Europe is generally considered to be the epicenter of climbing by bike and that reputation is well-deserved. Full of very steep roads often laid down before regular auto traffic was used on them, Europe does contain many difficult hill climbs along with having the distinction of being home to most of the major cycling tours. Because of this many climbs there are well known; not only to professional riders but also to the legions of amateur cyclists on the continent. As there are few major stage races in the United States, many of the best climbs are relatively unknown. However, the U.S. has a wide variety of climbs and a selection comparable to the most difficult used in the major Tours. Whiteface Mountain in New York for example is almost identical in length and grade (steepness) to the famous French climb of L'Alpe d'Huez, one that is often a stage finish in the Tour de France and considered among the toughest used in that race. Others such as Whitney Portal in California and Mount Equinox in Vermont are even more difficult. Owens Valley in California may have more beyond category climbs within its walls than any location on earth. Nearby Death Valley has multiple category 1 (the second most difficult classification) climbs by itself. There are many climbs with over 5,000 feet of vertical elevation gain, and others that top out in the rarified air above 10,000 feet, including the highest paved road outside of the Andes and Himalayan Mountains. The U.S. also has a select group of climbs that are among the most difficult in the world including Onion Valley Road in California, several Hawaiian giants, unique in that they gain up to and beyond 10,000 vertical feet of continuous climbing, and the incomparable Mount Washington in New Hampshire, which may be the toughest of them all.   Road bike cycling and hill climbing in particular are enjoying a surge in popularity in the U.S., perhaps due to the success of the major road bike races and Lance Armstrong and/or the ongoing fitness/physical challenge craze in this country. There are now many hill climb races throughout the country including one on Mount Washington which sells out very early each year despite a hefty entry fee. In spite of growing popularity however, there is little published information on the location of the best road bike hill climbs and very little accurate data on the length and elevation gain of these climbs. Many roads in the U.S. are hilly but that is not the intent of this guide. The location, description and profiling of major individual hills is its aim. As such, I set out to publish a guide for those cyclists looking for this information and to collect data for climb comparison purposes. You will have many of these hills all to yourself as the majority are not well known.

In addition to listing the location of America's major climbs I wanted to provide accurate data on their length, grade, elevation gain and other statistics which are generally lacking. While there are various regional data available it is important when compiling data to reduce the variability of measurement that can occur from multiple sources and to apply consistent definitions to hill climbs. The listed statistics for climbs often vary as different people use different starting and ending points and less than accurate measurement procedures. At times climb gradients are reported inaccurately or overestimated such as when the maximum grade is sometimes considered the average grade. In addition, climbs are sometimes profiled by using mapping software to analyze roads that have been superimposed upon a topographic map. Roads are at times not accurately laid down within map contours which can result in less than accurate measurements. The measurements in this guide were all obtained directly on each climb and compiled by one source.

There are thousands of climbs within the United States so obviously they all cannot be included in these pages. This means that many of the stout San Francisco Bay area climbs such as Quimby and Sierra Roads in California, the extremely scenic Logan Pass in Glacier National Park, Montana, many super steep hills such as Balcomb Canyon Road, Black Canyon Road, Iowa Hill Road and Fort Ross Road in California and Hurricane Mountain Road in New Hampshire, local icons Lookout and Cheyenne Mountains in Colorado and many others had to be left out. What this guidebook does include are the most difficult road bike climbs in the U.S. (see appendix for ranking of top 100). Other climbs are described due to a steep grade, high altitude attained and a small group with some other unique aspect such as outstanding scenery (along with significant climbing), cycling history or some combination of the above. Appendices in this guide rank climbs by overall difficulty, most difficult segments from 1/10th to ten miles, average grade (minimum 10%), summit elevation (minimum 10,000 feet), elevation gain (minimum 5,000 feet) and several other categories. The author has first hand knowledge of 137 out of the 144 (95%) described climbs in this guide. Climbs with estimated statistics are noted. Not all states are represented obviously and if a climb involves two or more states it is listed in the state where the climb terminates. It is a difficult task to attempt to record and document all of the significant climbs within the U.S. so if noteworthy ascents were left out please send the appropriate information to the author.

While some of the rides in this guide are for the serious road cyclist only, there are many moderate climbs for the rider looking to improve their climbing skills and/or fitness level. Be sure to know your fitness and ability level before you tackle the longer and/or more difficult hills in this book. Start with the shorter, less steep climbs and progress from there. As all are located in the mountains, the scenery along the way is usually spectacular and will help ease the pain of a tough ascent.

Defining a hill climb

Along with location and reporting more precise measurements on the length and elevation gained for selected climbs, this guide will attempt to standardize the definition of a hill climb. That is, what constitutes a climb, what are the starting and ending points and, if multiple approaches, the shortest route to the top. The author agrees with the Tour de France designation that true climbs need a minimum average grade of 4%. The start and finish of most climbs are generally easy to define as they have definite beginnings and endings. Others are a bit vague, particularly along shallow-grade stretches of road. The starting point of these types of climbs is considered to be the transition from flat to a definite climb or a significant change in elevation for very gently climbing stretches of roads. A good example of the latter is the north side of Red Mountain Pass in Colorado along Route 550 (one of the most spectacular climbs in the U.S.). Route 550 actually begins to climb many miles to the north of its listed start in Ouray, CO. However, the grade is so slight that the author believes this should not be considered a hill climb. Once in Ouray it is quite clear where the true hill begins as there is a significant change in grade right in the middle of town.

Another topic worthy of discussion regarding climb definitions is a clarification of their ending points. Most climbs have an easy-to-define end such as Mount Washington in New Hampshire or Mount Evans in Colorado, both of which dead-end very close to the top of the respective mountains. However, some do not. For climbs that do not dead end, the top is considered when the road descends from that point (such as mountain passes), or if it reaches a significant flat without significant climbing beyond it. A good example of the latter is Alternate 14 in Wyoming, one of the most difficult climbs in this guide. At its listed top the road flattens out. Over the next few miles the road rolls up and down before peaking at an altitude that is slightly higher than the listed climb peak. However, the additional climbing is not constant and is over such shallow grade that the additional riding does not constitute climbing in the author's mind.

Another issue in defining climbs is how flat sections and/or descents along the route factor in. A climb can have small flats and/or infrequent small descents and still be considered a continuous ascent as long as the vast majority of the route is uphill (< 10% of the route is flats/descents). Many major hill climbs have small descents along the way but these sections always lead to significant additional climbing. Some very good rides with serious elevation gain however contain multiple flats/descents and are not included. These would include both routes into Mountain Home State Forest in California and Chain of Craters Road/Mauna Loa East in Hawaii; very entertaining rides that climb significant distances but that have too much of their route along flat and/or descending terrain.

Some climbs may have a single major flat/descent (no more than one mile in length) if there is extended, significant climbing both before and after the flat/descent. For example, Mount Mitchell in North Carolina has a single major descent along its route but because there is significant climbing both before and after the descent it is considered a single climb. If a climb has more than one major flat/descent along its route it is considered two separate climbs. For instance, route 168 from Fresno to Kaiser Pass in California has more than 8000 feet of elevation gain along its route but there are several major descents along the way so the route is actually several different climbs. Mount Hamilton near San Jose, California is another example; it contains three uphill sections between two fairly major descents and while the climbing sections are worthy in themselves, the route from bottom to top is not considered by most to be one hill climb.

Some climbs, due to local routing or tradition (such as a race route), may at times be described with different beginning or ending points than this guide. However, the beginning, end and route of a climb should always ensure the shortest (and thus the steepest) path to the top. For example, the start of the north side of Mount Greylock in Massachusetts is often listed as within Heritage Park in North Adams, Massachusetts. This guide lists the start as the corner of Route 2 and Notch Road which results in the shortest, and thus overall steepest, route to the top.

Definitions of Terms

This guide will use several terms to describe each climb which are defined below:

Total elevation - This is the elevation gained in feet from the starting point to the top of the climb. If a climb has descents within it this additional climbing is not included in the total elevation gained. Elevations were measured using global positioning satellite (GPS) positions from which a very accurate elevation was then determined by plotting the fixed point using a topographic software program.

Length - This is the distance of the climb in miles. If you are retracing your route back to the starting point, in order to determine the total distance of the ride, simply double the climb's length. Climb lengths were measured by automobile odometer (at least two measures and averaged) and cycle computer where applicable.

Average Grade (maximum grade) - This is the average percent grade or steepness of the climb and is expressed as a percentage (8%). The grade assigned to each hill is the average grade over the entire climb. The higher the percent grade, the steeper the climb. Percent grade is determined by dividing the elevation gain by the length of the climb. The maximum grade is just that. The measured maximum gradient must extend all the way across the road (a very steep inside corner that could be bypassed for instance does not qualify) and be at least ten feet in length. Maximum gradient was measured by gradiometer. In the listed climb descriptions the distance and elevation data only reflect the contiguous portion of the road that is part of the climb. If the climb includes small flats or descents, they are included in the distance but do not contribute to the net elevation gain. Thus the average grade may not in some cases accurately represent the true nature of the climb. That is, there are usually sections on the climb that are steeper than the average grade along with sections that are less steep than the average grade.

Rating - There are several formulas available to rank climbs. All have shortcomings and have received criticism. In major races such as the Tour de France climbs are ranked using a numeric scale from 4 (easiest) to 1 with an extra classification describing the most difficult climbs as hors categoire or 'beyond category'. There are general guidelines for these categorizations that involve length and grade. However there are not precise definitions for each category and often the ratings are not applied consistently. In addition, climbs are often ranked according to their placement within a race stage meaning that a climb towards the end of a stage may be categorized as a 2 when the same climb may be a 3 (easier) if placed at the beginning of the stage. You may also have noticed that more recently certain climbs used in the Tour de France have been receiving a more difficult rating than for previous tours (call it hill inflation perhaps), regardless of their placement in a stage. The elevation reached within a climb is not taken into account in this and most other ratings systems as well. As increasing elevation has deleterious effects on physical performance, this factor should be taken into consideration. The point here is that a more accurate formula is needed and the one listed below is an attempt to more precisely quantify the difficulty of a climb and has taken into account the climb's elevation gain, average grade, altitude, surface and grade variability:

Square root of the average grade x total elevation gain x altitude adjustment (see altitude adjustment description) x surface adjustment (see surface adjustment description) x grade variability (see grade variability adjustment description).

      Altitude adjustment: Altitude research indicates that human performance shows a noticeable performance detriment beginning at approximately 2000 feet elevation of approximately 1% with subsequent performance deficits with increasing altitude and duration of activity. There are other elements that affect performance at altitude but vary by individual and at this point in time are very difficult if not impossible to quantify. The author acknowledges that the adjustment presented here is an estimation of the effects of altitude on performance.

      Surface adjustment: Determined by calculating the percentage of the climb that is non-paved and multiplying that by 0.25 (estimation that these unpaved surfaces are 25% more difficult to ride compared to paved surfaces). All of the hill climbs in this guide are 100% paved with the exception of Mount Washington in New Hampshire (21.3% unpaved), the east side of Figueroa Mountain Road in CA (9% unpaved) and Wildrose and Emigrant Pass West in CA (both 2% unpaved). These four climbs are included because the majority of the route and both the start and finish are paved, and the unpaved sections are packed down and easily ridden. The current surfaces of the paved roads in the guide are not adjusted because while older paved surfaces are more difficult to ride, almost all the roads in this guide are repaved at intervals.

      Grade variability adjustment: If a climb has two or more segments where the grade of the segment exceeds the average climb grade by at least five percentage points the rating is adjusted by 0.025 (assumption that grade variability results in a slightly more difficult climb) for each of those sections. Very few climbs meet this criterion.

As you can see from the climb rankings there is very little difference in the numeric rating of many of the climbs. So little in fact that you will have a very difficult time discerning the differences while on the bike. All that having been said, there are too many variables involved to precisely rank a climb numerically and it is not the main intent of this guide to do so. While the author believes this rating system is an improvement over other models it is hoped that these ratings, while serving as a general guide to compare climbs, will also serve to spur debate and perhaps eventually a more accurate rating system.

Directions - The starting point for almost all directions for climbs listed in this guidebook is the nearest town, some of which are very tiny places. A good road map will be helpful to locate and reach many of these locations. I would recommend the North American Road Atlas from AAA as it contains a town index for each state but any national highway road map will do.

Facilities - This is the closest town with adequate food, lodging and a bike shop. Often there are food and lodging (but not a bike shop) more closely available. These data are listed as of 2007 so keep in mind that things could change over time.

Airport - The closest major airport is defined as one providing daily jet service. For those equidistant from multiple airports, the largest is listed.

Rules of the Road

- Wear a helmet.
- Follow the same driving rules as motorists and be sure to obey all traffic patterns and road signs.
- Wear bright colors so you are more visible to motorists.
- Ride single file on busy roads so that motorized vehicles can pass.
- Use hand signals to alert motorists to your next move.
- Ride with traffic and not against it.
- Make eye contact with drivers and assume they do not see you.
- Try to avoid riding in foggy, rainy or windy conditions.
- Be alert for sewer grates, manhole covers, cattle guards, oily pavement, gravel, wet leaves and ice.
- Give parked cars a wide berth.
- Many of these listed climbs are fairly long rides so go prepared with an extra tube along with pump, tool kit, rain gear, food and plenty of fluids at all times.
- It is usually best to ride with a partner or partners. In case of emergency one rider can go for help if needed.
- Some of the climbs in this guide are closed by snow in winter (noted in climb descriptions). As the length of the season varies greatly at altitude, always call ahead in late Spring and Fall for possible road closures.

Pre-Ride Check:

- Check the tires for proper inflation.
- Check the brakes for proper traction.
- Check all quick releases to make sure they are tight.
- Check the chain for tightness.
- Check all nuts and bolts.
- Spin your wheels through frame and brakes.
- Make sure you have all necessary gear for the particular climb/ride.
- Bring a positive attitude along whenever possible.

Improving Climbing Ability

For new cyclists, hill climbing is one of the most daunting aspects of riding. More experienced cyclists, however, enjoy climbing and regard tough hills as a challenge. It is a great feeling to make a solid climb and then enjoy the descent down the other side. The simplest way to improve your climbing technique and the best training for climbing is to climb; that is, to incorporate hills into your rides. However, don't start climbing big hills until you have built up an adequate cycling fitness base. Try to accumulate a significant amount of relatively flat riding first. At that point add shorter/moderate grade hills to your rides and work your way up to the longer and/or steeper climbs. Incorporating hills in your riding will not make them any shorter but eventually they will feel that way.

Cycling Techniques for Climbing

Improving your basic cycling techniques can also improve your climbing ability. It is important to maintain a smooth, steady rhythm as you pedal up the hill. Unless very short in length, start a climb with as slow a pace as possible. This will allow you to develop a rhythm which not only includes the pedaling cadence but breathing as well. Breathe slowly and deeply as this will help establish a smooth pedaling cadence. Obviously in your pedal stroke it is much easier to apply force to the pedals when your foot is on the down stroke. However, this results in uneven power output contributing to slight accelerations and decelerations of the bike which becomes exaggerated when climbing. To remedy this try to lift your knee and drag your foot backwards across the bottom of the pedal stroke, pulling upwards slightly on the upstroke and pulling the pedal forward across the top of its rotation.

There are several other factors to consider when climbing. First, make sure you have the right gears. At least a 39-tooth small chain ring in front and a 25-tooth rear gear (a 27 or 28 is even better if you will be riding consistently on steep hills). Upon encountering a hill, do not shift too soon as this can result in a momentum loss from a high RPM spinning effect. Conversely, you must not end up in a gear that is too large which tends to tire the rider out. The proper climbing cadence varies among individuals. The idea with gearing is to maintain a cadence that is comfortable, shifting as you tire and the RPM's start to drop. Basically, if the gradient varies on the climb adjust your gearing so that your cadence and level of effort are maximized.

Another factor is whether to sit or stand during the ascent. Seated is more energy efficient but a standing position can produce much more power. A simple rule to start with is that if the hill is long, climb in the saddle, and if short or while attacking, stand. Reality dictates that on most challenging hills you will do both. For most of the climb you will find it is more efficient to sit in the saddle. Put your hands on the top of the brake hoods or handlebars and keep them relaxed. Try to change their positioning periodically. The upper body should not be crunched forward too far and the shoulders should be open. This will allow for easier breathing as the climb continues. Relax your upper body as well, as this will decrease oxygen demands. Your weight should be over the cranks to maximize power during the pedal stroke. Try not to bounce on the pedals as you shift from side to side. Developing a rhythm that combines pedaling and breathing will make a big difference in your climbing efficiency. At times you will need to stand such as on very steep sections or when sprinting past a fellow rider. Just before you stand, shift to a higher gear as you can generate more power in this position (shift back when you sit down again). As you come off of the saddle continue with an even pedal stroke and push your hands forward. Come out of the saddle on the down stroke to minimize loss of momentum.

Specific Training for Hill Climbing

While the physiology of human performance training is much more understood today than in the past, training is still as much art as science. That is, there is more than one way to improve performance. However, perhaps the more important considerations are time and commitment. Time to train is obviously limited for most. With that in mind it is paramount that this limited time is put to good use. Intensity is the key with adequate rest for recovery. Particularly with hill climbing which involves very intense bursts of effort, adequate recovery is essential to avoid overtraining and burnout. In addition, train consistently for best results. Develop specific climbing goals and a plan to reach those goals. Listen to your body and back off if needed. Commit to climbing success and it will likely follow.

Good climbers have certain attributes that contribute to their success. All have an endurance base and have developed solid power to weight ratios which gives the ability to generate greater amounts of force with each pedal stroke. They also have high anaerobic endurance which results in greater levels of lactic acid tolerance. Training to improve climbing ability should focus on these physiologic aspects.

Build a Base

As previously mentioned make sure you have a solid cycling base before adding significant climbing to your riding and attempting the interval routines described later in this section. You should complete many miles of distance riding on mostly flat terrain to build your endurance base before moving on to more specialized routines that target climbing ability. The amount of time needed will vary by individual, ranging from several months to several years of regular road cycling depending on age, health and fitness level. After a period of mainly flat riding, add moderate hills to your regular endurance rides. As you progress, add longer and steeper hills.

Power to Weight Ratio

Climbing ability has a strong correlation with power to weight ratio; in fact it is perhaps the most accurate predictor of climbing success. As you may have noticed, the climbing specialists on the pro tour are almost all very lean (the late Marco Pantani comes to mind). Thus, climbing can be improved by increasing power, losing body weight or, for the greatest results, a combination of the two. Even a relatively small weight loss (3-5 lbs) can produce significant improvement. Much information is available regarding losing weight so this guide will not attempt to add to that body of knowledge. Just keep in mind that weight loss can lead to reductions in power output (to maintain power lose as much fat and as little muscle as possible). Increasing cycling power will be touched upon in the following sections and comes about through specific training.

Regarding the advantages of lower weight, do not forget your bike. As long as component stiffness is not compromised (stiffer rims and frames flex less during use and thus take less energy to push up hills) reducing your machine's weight will improve its ability to climb as well. Rotating weight is the real key so you will see the biggest gains from reductions in this area. Use the lightest rims, pedals and shoes you can afford. Tires with smoother and thinner treads and stronger sidewalls will also help.

Improving Lactate Threshold

Lactate threshold is the point at which lactic acid begins to accumulate above moderate levels, resulting in fatigue in the affected muscles. This quickly results in the inability to continue to perform at this level of work. Most riders know the heavy legged feeling after a hard bout of work when you must slow down in order to keep going. The goal of training is to raise the point at which lactic acid accumulates enough to affect performance. All things being equal, the higher your lactate threshold, the faster the pace you can hold on climbs. While lactate threshold can be measured directly it correlates well with heart rate and is normally between 75-90% of maximum heart rate. The goal of climbing-specific training should be to increase that percentage towards the top of the range. A simple way to estimate your lactate threshold is to perform two bouts of work. When rested and motivated and after a good warm-up, perform a twenty minute time trial at **maximum** effort and record your average heart rate. Repeat this test under similar conditions. The average heart rate for both efforts is a close approximation of your heart rate at your lactate threshold. Providing you have a sufficient aerobic endurance base (see 'Build a Base' above) lactate threshold training should improve your climbing ability. This is very demanding training however and will require proper recovery between bouts so don't forget to include easy days on the bike when needed.

Interval Routines

A very effective way to increase your power and to raise your lactate threshold in order to improve climbing ability is through the use of intervals. Intervals are relatively short bursts of more intense effort followed by a recovery period. Several of the below routines should be interspersed (start at the top of the below list and progress down) within your regular riding training (1-3 times per week) depending upon the season. Use them more frequently for pre-season training; tapering off before races. Add/delete routines as needed. Recovery between intervals should be easy, high cadence spinning on mostly level ground.

Big gear climbs - On various hill grades shift up one cog from normal (harder gear) for 1-2 minutes. Keep cadence at least 50 RPM and stay seated.

Cruise intervals - 3 to 5 intervals for 6-12 minutes each on a moderate grade (3-5%) at or just below your lactate threshold. Recover for 2-4 minutes. Gradually add minutes to each interval.

Anaerobic endurance intervals - 3-5 intervals for 2-4 minutes each on a 6-8% grade, gradually building the intensity, with cadence of at least 60 RPM. Intensity should be above your lactate threshold for the second half of the interval. Recovery should be double the interval length.

Extended Climbing at Lactate Threshold - On a steady and moderate grade, climb for 15-30 minutes at or just slightly above your lactate threshold. Gradually add minutes up to 30 (or the longest hill you may need to climb).

Sit/Stand intervals - On a moderate hill and at a comfortable cadence, alternate seated and standing climbing of equal intervals. After thirty seconds in the saddle, stand on the pedals for 30 seconds. After another minute of climbing in the saddle, stand for one minute, etc. Gradually build the intervals up to 4-5 minutes each.

Hill Sprints - Perform 5-10 sprints for 10-15 seconds at maximum effort. Gradually move from moderate to steeper hills. Recover for five minutes between each sprint.

Hill Jumps - While climbing a moderate hill do 4-5 sets of 3-5 jumps for ten crank turns (both feet) at maximum effort. Recover for one minute between each jump and five minutes between each set.

Advanced Hill Jumps - On a moderate grade perform 3-5 two minute sets, attacking every thirty seconds for ten pedal strokes. Stand for the attacks which should be at maximum effort; stay seated otherwise. Recover for five minutes between sets.

Weight Training

One factor linked to climbing success is leg strength. Particularly if you cannot put in year round riding on hills, weight training sessions should be added to your weekly routine. Ideally hit the weight room 2-3 times per week in the off season and once per week in season, tapering off before races or big rides. Increasing upper body strength has the potential to reduce upper body fatigue and increasing lower body strength will give you the ability to push

The very difficult west side of Townes Pass in Death Valley, CA

Riding the Rockies

a bigger gear over the same hill. The below exercises will give you the most benefit for your time spent in the gym. Do not include both squats and leg presses unless leg strength is a very weak area. Masters riders or those with lower back issues should not include squats in their routine and should perform the leg press instead.

Squat - 2-3 sets of 8-12 repetitions

Leg press - 2-3 sets of 8-12 repetitions

Calf raise - 2-3 sets of 8-12 repetitions

Step-ups - 2-3 sets of 8-12 repetitions

Bench press - 2-3 sets of 8-12 repetitions

Lat pulldown - 2-3 sets of 8-12 repetitions

Push-ups - 2-3 sets of 25 repetitions

Sit-ups (crunches) - 2-3 sets of 25 repetitions

Back extensions - 2-3 sets of 25 repetitions

Descending Skills

Descending ability, like any other skill, is best obtained and improved with practice. The more time you can spend on descending, the more confidence and speed you will be able to develop. The most important aspect of descending is relaxation. Anxiety can narrow your concentration and you may end up missing a dangerous aspect of the road ahead. Speed is obviously important but pushing your speed to the point of fear will not help your descending skills. Work on relaxation and speed will follow. Keep a slight bend in the arms and slide back in the saddle, keeping your hands on the drops of your bars. One important riding habit to develop is to look far enough in front of you to match the pace at which you are descending. During a faster descent you need to watch the road much further in front of the bike. Set up well in advance of a curve and do whatever braking needs to done before entering the turn. If you are riding in a group, spread out. This will allow each rider to take their preferred line through the corners; critical in that you may not have time to adjust once you commit. It also allows a greater margin if a rider needs to brake. For long descents you should use both brakes equally. Once in a turn any traction used for braking significantly reduces the traction available for cornering. In wet conditions the distance required to stop is extended. Lightly apply the brakes periodically on a wet descent to remove excess water from the rims. Compete only against yourself on a fast descent and exercise caution on unfamiliar roads by always being prepared for road debris or traffic around every blind corner. In many cases descents are followed by another climb; if so, try to spin the pedals as you approach the bottom so that you will be warmed up for the next section of riding. Take it easy, relax, concentrate on the road, and most importantly, practice descending, and you will find your skills improving.

Mental Training

As professional cyclist Chris Boardman once said "The best climbers do not suffer less, they just suffer faster". Climbing is painful, suffering the name of the game. That said there may also be some less conventional ways to improve your climbing ability. Developing mental focus to enable one to block out distractions, including physical discomfort, is another attribute of good climbers and should be included in your training regimen. All negative thoughts must go during workouts or races. The minute you think you cannot make a climb is when you may get dropped. Many riders are dropped on climbs before they reach their physical breaking point simply because of negative thoughts.

Begin working on mental focus by clearing your mind entirely. This can be a difficult skill to master but can be developed in stretches during long rides. Be patient as it sometimes takes time to see progress. Once this skill is developed begin to think of a single thought or image. Try to keep this single thought or image in your mind for extended periods. Once you have developed this ability you will find it much easier to concentrate over a climb. Work on visualizing images of light or soaring objects as you work your way up the hill. These images can lower the perception of effort. Even if climbing times are similar the effect should be one of additional energy for the remainder of the race or ride. Remember, everyone suffers on a tough climb. Climbing can be as much a mental as physical challenge, so try not to let a lack of self-confidence affect your performance. Developing ways to deal mentally with the physical aspects of getting over tough hills should produce better results on the road.

Climbing Tactics

There are some specific strategies regarding climbing that can have dramatic results when it comes to better race finishes. First of all, as with the overall route, it pays to be very familiar with the climbs along the way, so scout major hills if at all possible, noting the position of flat or very steep sections, particularly those that are stage/race finishes. When many inexperienced riders come to a hill they simply go all out and feel tremendous pressure to reach the top. Unless it is the last climb of the day doing so results in spending enormous amounts of energy that could be saved for the finish. Until you are a great climber you should maintain your own pace. Trying to stay with the top climbers is not good strategy. Instead try to find the exact personal pace that will help you cut your losses. Never ride faster than you know you can go. If needed, as you get comfortable with the climb, see if you can pick up the pace over the last half so that by the top you can catch the original group with which you started. You may be surprised by how many riders you pass along the way. Ideally try to time the effort so that you catch the pack at the summit. Unless you are the first over the top, be careful not to slow down near summits that are not race finishes. As the leaders begin to accelerate on the descent each rider has to push harder over the top in order to hold the wheel in front of him. Shift into a bigger gear as you approach the summit and accelerate over the top. You can recover on the descent from the extra effort involved.

Riders who are good sprinters often come to a hill in or near the lead and then drift to the back of the pack during the climb. On the descent and any following flats they can often catch the lead group before the next climb. By doing this several times early in a ride/race you can save a lot of energy for the finish while also developing the confidence of knowing that you do not have to crest climbs near the front to be successful. If the climb is the last of the day, obviously your tactics will need to change. You may need to make an all out effort to catch the lead group such as when the finish is very close or if being with the group will save a lot of energy (long, flat section just ahead). As you gain experience and become more aware of group dynamics you will start to make better decisions earlier in a climb and save energy as well.

Once you become a good climber, attack on the hills. Use your strength to put time on your competitors as you may need it over the remainder of the race/ride. An early attack can keep pressure on those who may be stronger in other areas. Riders that push too hard trying to keep up with you on a hill early in the race may find themselves struggling on the last climb of the day. Steeper sections are often a good place to launch an attack as you can more quickly open a gap before other riders react. However, attacking early on a hilly stage is a risky decision as you will either ride to victory or go down in flames if the peloton swallows you up before the finish. Depending on the result your decision will be portrayed as courageous or foolish bravado so if you go make sure you are committed to the move. Many a cyclist has made a name for themselves breaking away on a monster climb and staying away so don't let a prior failed attempt keep you from trying again.

If the race finish is the hill crest obviously it is best to be out in front by a comfortable margin and cruise to victory up the final climb. However, until you are a super climber that situation may rarely present itself. Unless it is a very long climb get into the lead group as soon as possible. Once there, knowing when to attack is a crucial skill to master. Much of your decision will be based on how you are feeling that day and on race conditions and will become clearer with additional climbing/racing experience. The other contending riders may also come into play. If there is a sprinter in the lead group you may want to go early and take his legs out from under him. If so, take a measured approach. Launch an attack but not an all out effort. Even though part of the group may stay with you, the effort should drop a few riders. If you are feeling good continue the attack. If you are able to continue at a relatively high cadence you should drop all but the strongest climbers. Unless you have ridden all riders off of your wheel it will come down to your placement in the group and timing as the finish line draws near. The first thing you must do is know where the finish line is. If you scouted the hill even if the last section is twisty with obscured views you should have an advantage. Once you have a good idea of how far away the line is, positioning will be key. Draft off other riders as much as possible as you approach the summit. When the finish is in sight try to be the second or third wheel before the final sprint begins. Realize this is easier said than done and knowing how to position within the group will again come from experience. The time to start your finishing sprint will depend upon your sprinting ability. The greater your sprinting skills, the earlier you can launch your assault. Always be alert for the rider in front of you moving first. Come out of the saddle on the down stroke as you make your move. Once you pull away try to stay directly in front of the rest of the pack so they will have to move around you to pass. Don't look back as you power toward the line. All of these actions should be thought out well before the actual finishing stretch. Many of these tactical maneuvers come with experience so train with experienced riders to see how they approach climbs, or shadow a particular rider, noting how they adjust to different situations on the hill.

Summary

To get the most out of the time on your bike and to avoid overtraining refer to the below summary:

- Build a strong aerobic base before adding a lot of climbing mileage to your training rides
- Add climbing to your regular training rides
- Utilize interval training to improve climbing ability
- Build up the intensity of your training slowly
- Train consistently for best results
- Eat a balanced diet
- Try to get a minimum of eight hours sleep every night
- Set short, medium and long-term goals
- Use a training diary and review when needed
- Know yourself and adjust your workouts accordingly
- Don't forget to include easy days on the bike if you are including extensive climbing routines in your training
- Use mental techniques to develop positive thoughts during climbing
- Practice descending skills to round out your mountain training
- Don't forget the tactical side of climbing

Memorable Climbing Performances

There have been many amazing climbing performances over the years, the most publicized having taken place in Europe. These performances are too numerous to list here and are well documented in other places. From the dominating mountain stage wins of Alfredo Binda, Gino Bartali, Fausto Coppi and Charly Gaul in the early European tours to the death of Tim Simpson on Mount Venous and other more contemporary battles among the legends of the sport including Eddy Merckx, Bernard Hinault, Greg Lemond, Marco Pantani and Lance Armstrong, there are many stories to tell. Exclusively American climbing exploits have a fairly short, but accomplished history, mainly contained within the last thirty years or so. The stories presented here have an American theme (either by rider or location) and while some are well known many may be unknown to all but the most die-hard cycling fan.

There are so many tales to tell that all cannot be expanded upon, including some of the early Red Zinger/Coors Classic stage race battles in the Rockies, European race exploits such as Greg Lemond's wins in the 1980 Circuit de la Sarthe and 1983 World Championship, Alexi Grewal's mountain stage win in the 1984 Tour de l'Avenir, the 1986 and 1987 Tour of Switzerland wins over difficult terrain by Andy Hampsten, and the Blue Ridge and Appalachian Mountain performances in the now defunct Tour du Pont. Others worthy of mention but not included in these pages are the victories by Moninger, Vaughters and Wherry in the now defunct Red Zinger/Saturn Classic, one of the most difficult one day races in the world (held in Colorado from 2000-2002), Lance Armstrong's uphill time trial win to capture the 2001 Tour of Switzerland, his queen (most difficult) stage win in the 2001 Tour de France that gave him the overall race lead or the two mountain stage victories that contributed mightily to his 2002 TdF win. In addition, the exploits of climbers in the recently inaugurated Everest Challenge, a two day stage race in California that has the greatest elevation to mileage ratio for any U.S. race, are not touched upon as well as many others due to lack of space or detailed information. Listed chronologically, those listed here are performances that are among the most significant in American cycling climbing history.

Top of the World

Mount Evans in Colorado is one of the most difficult hill climbs in the world. With a beginning elevation well above 7000 feet, the paved road on its slopes reaches heights greater than any outside of the Himalayas or Andes Mountains. It is also home to the oldest climbing race in the U.S., first held in 1962. Winning this very difficult race, with its unparalleled altitude attained, is a testament to climbing ability. The winner list is one of great American climbers and includes Alexi Grewal, Ned Overend, Jonathan Vaughters, and Tom Danielson. One win in this prestigious event would be a worthy achievement for any top level rider. Multiple wins signify a truly great climber. Winning the overall title each time it was held from 1975-1980, American Bob Cook also set the course record four times in that span. Tragically, Bob Cook passed away in 1981 at the age of twenty-three. The race is now named in memorial for the first five time winner of the event who many consider perhaps the best American climber of any era. Mike Engleman also won the race five times in a row from 1991 to 1995, an equally incredible feat. Scott Moninger has won this race an amazing six times which is quite an achievement. Winning this difficult race multiple times deserves to be considered among the most impressive of climbing feats.

Rocky Mountain High

The Coors Classic (formerly the Red Zinger Classic) was America's first top level stage race and one of the most influential cycling events on this continent. Attracting the world's best riders, it allowed many Americans to see top flight competitive cycling for the first time. Held mainly in Colorado, it always contained many hill climbs within a high altitude environment.

In the 1981 version the top team entered was from the Soviet Union. Even though they were technically an amateur team (members did not receive any prize money but were fully supported by the Soviet government and thus could train full time) they were as good as the best professional teams of that era. This was evident in the precise teamwork of its cyclists. Once the Soviet train got moving and was working at its peak it was riding everyone off of its wheels. However, there was one exception. A young man from Nevada who was just starting to make waves in the cycling world was also entered in the Coors Classic that year. Having won several prestigious American titles, he was able to stay with the Soviets, and any other riders for that matter, through the difficult terrain. Greg Lemond, despite having a weak team, stayed with the mighty Soviets throughout the high altitude rides and climbs of the Rockies, pulling ahead at the end of several stages to win. Essentially winning the race single handedly, his impressive mountain performance was a prelude to major tour victories on cycling's most hallowed grounds.

The Future

The Tour de l'Avenir (Tour of the Future) held in France each year is a 10-day stage race sponsored by the Tour de France for top amateurs and young professional riders. It is also similar to the TdF in that it contains plenty of climbing and top flight competition. In 1982 the field was one of the strongest ever including the best national teams in the world along with some of the top up and coming European pros. In addition, a team from Columbia was entered that contained some of the best climbers on the planet. The team from East Germany dominated the early, flat stages but things began to change in Stage 4. This stage was a short mountain time trial and it was here that that the future arrived as American Greg Lemond rode to victory, picking up eighteen seconds on the second place rider. The next day's stage was a brutal one including climb after climb along the route and ending with a hilltop finish. The Columbian team attacked early and often but Lemond followed each one. Toward the end of the stage he opened up a gear that would later be seen winning the Tour de France as he pulled away from everyone and crushed the stage, winning by over five minutes. Greg Lemond ended up winning the Tour de l'Avenir by more than ten minutes, becoming the first and only American ever to do so and building on a record that would become one of the best in the history of the sport.

The Women's Movement

In 1984 the Tour de France held the first Tour for women. Because of the Olympics being held in Los Angeles later that summer the U.S. did not send an official team (and its best riders) to the event. Instead a bicycle club from New Jersey sent a small group to represent the country. Without a coach or national uniforms (they also rode on borrowed bikes) the group headed to France not without a bit of trepidation. Once the race began over mostly flat stages, the Tour was dominated by a strong Dutch team. The last rider picked for the American effort, Marianne Martin, used these early stages to ride herself into top shape. By the time Stage 14 rolled around Martin was ready to make her move. The stage was a difficult one, essentially one long hill and ending at the top of a ski resort. Martin pulled away right from the start and went on to win the stage by almost four minutes, an amazing margin of victory considering the stage was only twenty miles long. Picking up the yellow jersey as race leader as well at the end of that day, she held on all the way to Paris to become the first winner of the Tour de France Feminin.

Conquering the Colombian Heights

Despite its endemic poverty and violence, the country of Colombia, with its towering mountains, has somehow managed to produce a storied cycling history. With some of the toughest riding conditions in the world it is a very inhospitable place for foreign riders; rebuffing even the great Fausto Coppi late in his career. Full of very high elevation passes as well as many of the best climbers in the world (in fact, Colombian Luis Herrera is the only rider to win the King of the Mountains title outright in all three major tours), Colombia held the annual Caracol de la Montana stage race and billed it as the unofficial world championship of climbing. In 1985, battling the altitude and humidity, American Andy Hampsten put in a amazing climbing performance, beating the conditions and competition to come away with the race victory and continuing a series of major American climbing exploits against the best riders in the world.

The American Advance

By 1986 the great French rider, Bernard Hinault, had won five Tours de France and was the dominant rider of his generation. After publicly stating that he would support Greg Lemond in the 1986 TdF, Hinault held a one minute lead on his young teammate in that year's race entering the Pyrenees Mountains. The next day Hinault attacked, and Lemond, very frustrated in the domestique role, could not follow, giving up almost another five minutes by the end of the stage. The following day started as a repeat of the previous one as Hinault again went to the front. On the last climb of the day the race leaders, including Hinault and Lemond, were in the lead group. Multiple attacks were launched and this time Lemond did not hold back. With help from teammate Andy Hampsten, Lemond broke away early on the climb and, pulling away from Hampsten, crushed the stage, picking up almost all of the time he had lost to Hinault the day before. Showing he was now the best rider in the world, Lemond went on to win the Tour, becoming the first American to do so.

Italy Finally Falls

The Giro d'Italia is Italy's grand cycling tour. With a storied history it is the second most difficult race in the world to win. Italy has perhaps the toughest road climbs in Europe but if not, it certainly has more difficult climbs to include in its stages compared to the other major tours, and they are often put to good use. In 1988, Andy Hampsten was riding well as the Giro began. After a solid finish in the opening stage time trial the American hung around until the hills, gradually moving up in general classification. On Stage 12, the first with a hill finish, Hampsten won and put himself very close to the overall lead. The Giro was in the mountains at this point and Stage 14 would be a turning point. The big climb on that stage was up Gavia Pass, a very high, steep and difficult hill. In a pouring rain the peloton stayed together until the base of the Gavia and at that point no one knew what awaited up above on its cruel slopes. As the riders attacked the hill the rain turned to sleet and then to snow near the top. Hampsten stayed with the lead group as riders were shredded around him by the hill and the weather, many abandoning the stage. Hampsten, familiar with the conditions from his training days in Colorado, gritted his teeth and kept pumping the pedals, eventually finishing second in the stage but taking the overall race lead and putting all but one rider minutes behind him in the general classification. He survived multiple attacks over the last week of the race and then won the mountain time trial at the end to cruise to victory, becoming the first and only American to win the Giro d'Italia.

To Descend One Must Climb

After Greg Lemond's dominating win in the 1986 Tour de France the terrible story of his hunting accident is well known, an event that kept him off the bike and on the sidelines for nearly two years. Who knows what his already solid legacy may have been had he been healthy (and had he not had to endure several TdFs as a domestique to the great Bernard Hinault). With his performance capacity obviously diminished after the accident, he put on an amazing time trialing exhibition to win the 1989 Tour, performing well but not superbly in the mountains. In the 1990 TdF the same circumstances were present; Lemond was fit and able but still not quite his old self. The days of his physical domination over, he would need to win races not by brawn but by brains and will. Heading into the key stage in the Pyrenees just over halfway through the race, Lemond found himself behind Italy's Claudio Chiappucci by almost three minutes. As the mountain stages were almost over it was now or never if an assault on a third TdF was to be undertaken. The stage contained three giant climbs lined up over the last half of the route. Chiappucci attacked right at the base of the first climb and flew away, opening a big lead at the summit and increasing it, halfway up the next climb, the mighty Tourmalet, to over three minutes for the stage and almost six minutes overall. Realizing that a critical point had been reached, Lemond launched a severe attack up the Tourmalet, halving the gap to Chiappucci by the summit. The descent of the Tourmalet is a long one, twisting down through very dangerous turns. Always known as a good bike handler, Lemond came down the Tourmalet like a bat out of hell and by the bottom had caught Chiappucci! Making up a gap of one and a half minutes on a descent over another top professional bike rider is an amazing feat, and highlights the importance of descending in mountain stages. However, while catching the stage leader was a heroic effort there were still over eight miles of climbing yet to come before the finish and Chiapucci still had a large overall race lead. The small leading group headed up the final hill and stayed together over much of the final climb. With two miles remaining to the summit however another rider in the group attacked and Lemond went with him, dropping Chiappucci. The smaller group drove hard to the finish, dropping all but two riders by the end (Lemond and future five time TdF winner Miguel Indurain). By the finish Lemond had picked up almost three minutes on the race leader, cutting the overall lead to five seconds, a margin he could easily pick up during the last time trial stage before the race finish in Paris. Going on to win his third TdF, Lemond won the race on the slopes of the Pyrenees with an amazing climbing performance.

The Alp

First used in the Tour de France in 1952, L'Alpe d'Huez, with its multiple, numbered switchbacks, has become one of the most recognizable climbs in the world. Often used as a stage finish, the climb may be the true symbol of the Tour as decisive moments are often played out on its slopes. Almost mythic in stature, all of cycling's greats have done battle there and winning a stage atop the legendary Alp has become one of the most revered accomplishments in cycling. While certainly performing well at the highest level of the sport, Andy Hampsten came to the 1992 TdF without a top level result that matched the climbing exploits that led to his 1988 win in the Giro d'Italia. The Alps that year contained perhaps the most difficult stage of the race, containing four major climbs and ending on top of L'Alpe d'Huez. Feeling well that day, something stirred in Hampsten as he ascended the third climb of the day. Breaking away in a small group, they opened a gap on the field and descended toward L'Alpe. By the base of the climb the group had a four minute lead on everyone else. By the first of many hairpin turns Hampsten was alone. Using an increasingly larger gear he charged up the hill through the huge crowds, gradually pulling away and winning the stage. By conquering the legendary climb he joined cycling's legends on perhaps its most prized summit.

Mount Washington Falls

Mount Washington in New Hampshire may be the toughest climb in the world, with an average grade of almost 12% and portions of the route unpaved. The climb is a brutal one with no flats or descents to catch your breath and riders must often battle cold temperatures and howling winds. An annual hill climb race has been held on its slopes for many years, with the record for the climb having been set way back in 1980. The record stood for seventeen years until a young professional rider, Tyler Hamilton, arrived in 1997 and crushed the competition, lowering the record by almost six minutes in the process, a huge percentage decrease. The record has been lowered subsequently by small margins but Hamilton set the stage and drew attention, as well as some of the world's top riders, to what now may be the most coveted prize in American cycling climbing.

The giant switchbacks of Horseshoe Meadows Rd. loom over Owens Valley

A big mountain switchback

Ventoux

Often used in stage races, Mont Ventoux is a beast of a climb, perhaps the most difficult in France. Soon after the climb begins the trees and most vegetation disappear and riders are left stuck in a barren, parched moonscape that seems to sap the energy of anyone that moves through it. Often used in major European races such as the Dauphine Libere, a major stage race held the month before the Tour de France, Mont Ventoux is a climb that is feared by all riders. Many use the Dauphine as preparation for the Tour so Ventoux has been graced by all of cycling's greats through the years with many a heroic battle having been fought on its slopes, including the death of pro Tom Simpson in 1967 and a memorable duel between Lance Armstrong and Marco Pantani in the 2000 Tour de France. In fact the mountain became Armstrong's nemesis as he failed to win a race that ended on its slopes. The record for the climb had been set way back in 1955 by the great Charley Gaul, a TdF and Giro d'Italia winner with the nickname 'the angel of the mountains'. In 1999 the Dauphine included a time trial up Ventoux for Stage 3. As horrible as the mountain is within the peloton, it is even worse during a time trial. All alone against the hill, riders must dig deep and find an unaided way to the top. American Jonathan Vaughters came to the starting gate that day feeling pretty good. A very successful pro, he entered the stage close to the overall lead and felt a big move on Ventoux could be the difference between winning and losing the race. Vaughters attacked the hill from the beginning, gradually putting time on his opponents at each time check and won the stage, breaking the 44-year-old record for the climb.

A New Beginning

Many questions surrounded Lance Armstrong when the 1999 Tour de France began, including his ability to compete for one, having come back to the sport after a vicious battle with cancer (although that question had been answered with some success in pre Tour races). A second question was his ability to climb. A big time trial win early in the race had given him the overall lead as the peloton headed into the Alps. Skeptics were noting however that it was very unlikely that the American could continue his success into the big mountains of the tour. Never a great climber before his illness surely he would succumb once the roads tilted upward. The ninth stage of that year's race was a brutal one. It included six major climbs including the beyond category Galibier in France and Sestrieres in Italy, hallowed ground where all of cycling's greats had battled over the years. To make things worse the weather was poor that day so that the upper altitudes were shrouded in cold and wet weather. In the small lead group at the base of the last climb of the day were many of the best climbers in the race. As they ascended, several fell away so that only four remained. With three miles to go Armstrong attacked, opening a small gap. As the gap grew he poured it on in such a way that no one could respond, pulling away to win the stage by thirty-one seconds and widening his race lead over the top contenders to an almost insurmountable margin. Having dropped almost fifteen pounds and recovered his power since his illness, Armstrong had turned himself into a climbing machine. If there was any doubt regarding his abilities to climb the biggest mountains it was now gone as he went on to win his first TdF.

It Was No Fluke

Before the 2000 Tour de France many cycling pundits felt that Lance Armstrong's 1999 Tour win was a fluke of sorts. With several of the best riders absent that year they reasoned, he would be unlikely to repeat as champion in 2000 when the field included all of the top contenders. As the 2000 event got underway Lance soon found himself down by a wide margin in the overall classification and with a small lead over those considered his strongest competition. A few days later the Tour entered the mountains for the first time and with that a chance for riders to make a big move on the leader board. As the last climb of the day got underway in cold and rainy conditions up the Hautacam, a tough climb in the Pyrenees Mountains, the leading group contained many race contenders with several of them out ahead due to an early breakaway. Soon the group was attacked by 1998 Tour winner Marco Pantani, one of those absent from the 1999 Tour. Armstrong quickly closed the gap, in the process dropping several, among them Jan Ullrich, the 1997 TdF winner and another rider absent in 1999. Even on a very strong day it is a difficult thing for a cyclist to push an attack early on a climb. It is best to wait to see what shakes out as the finish line gets closer. An early attack is considered either foolish bravado or a heroic act depending upon the outcome. However, on that day Armstrong's instincts proved the better of conventional cycling wisdom. Once he had caught and passed Pantani he actually picked up the tempo and pulled away. The rest of the group could not respond and disappeared backward as Lance flew up the mountain. Continuing to charge to the finish line in a steady rain Armstrong caught all but one of the early breakaway riders. But more importantly he had put serious time on all of the top contenders, picking up anywhere from three to five minutes on each. While there was much more riding to be done, the Tour was essentially over and Armstrong had answered one more question.

Changing of the Guard Delayed

Jeannie Longo, an eleven time world champion, came to New Hampshire from France in 2000 looking for a different kind of challenge. Up against the defending women's champion, 18-year-old Genevieve Jeansson of Canada, and perhaps the hardest climb on earth, Mount Washington, Longo knew that she had her work cut out for her during the annual hillclimb race up its slopes. As the race begun, Jeansson took a forty second lead at the two mile mark as the climb headed into its steepest miles. Longo's experience began to show however as she gradually picked up the pace, catching Jeansson at four miles and opening a gap. Jeansson fought back and attacked but she could not quite close to the leader. Longo pulled away, opening a two minute lead and, in what is one of the most amazing climbing performances of all time, at forty-one years of age, won the race, passing all but the two top men and setting the women's record for the hill in the process.

The Look

In the 2001 Tour de France Lance Armstrong, having won the previous two Tours, was in a battle with German rider Jan Ullrich, a former Tour winner and his biggest threat to another victory, as the race entered the first mountain stage. The stage contained three beyond category climbs, ending on the top of the third, the famous L'Alpe d'Huez. Over the first two monster climbs, the Col de la Madeleine and the Col du Glandon, Armstrong struggled just to stay at the back of the lead group. At the beginning of the climb up L'Alpe, Ullrich and several teammates led the way. Suddenly Armstrong shot to the front, pulled there by his teammate Jose Luis Rubiero. As Rubiero pulled off and with Ullrich on his wheel, Armstrong came out of the saddle, and in a moment that has become one of the greatest in cycling history, turned to look back at his competition for a long moment, and accelerated away. Ullrich and the rest of the field had no response and Armstrong won the stage, picking up two minutes on his main rival on the way to his third Tour victory and further cementing his place in the folklore of cycling history.

Redemption

Perhaps driven by her loss to Jeannie Longo of France two years before, Canadian Genevieve Jeansson came to Mount Washington in 2002 with something to prove. The annual hillclimb race up its slopes is perhaps the most brutal on earth but no doubt having lost the event to someone more than twice her age in 2000 must have been incentive enough to draw her back again. She exploded up the hill right from the start, putting time on all of her competition. The road up Mount Washington never wavers and neither did Jeansson that day as she continued her torrid pace all the way to the top, winning the race by a margin of over ten minutes and breaking the hillclimb record previously held by Longo by over four minutes. Only two male riders finished ahead of her as she set a standard that has not since been approached and may be difficult to surpass.

The 'Off' Year

2003 is a year that Lance Armstrong and cycling fans will not forget. It was the year that almost wasn't; the year that Lance could be beaten. Struggling somewhat through the first half of the race Armstrong found himself with a slim lead as the first individual time trial approached. His lead due mostly to a winning team time trial performance, even Armstrong himself knew that something wasn't quite right that year. His pulls were not quite as they had been in years past and his race leading margin showed it. In the time trial Armstrong suffered, whether from mistakes or lack of preparation, and German Jan Ullrich, Lance's chief rival and in second place overall, did what had not been done in a major tour since 1996 as he put hurt and time on the Texas rider and trimmed his slim overall race lead to seconds. Armstrong looked like a beaten man and with only a fifteen second lead most believed that this was the time that he would finally fall as the tour headed into the Pyrenees and the toughest stage of the tour. Containing a category 1 and two beyond category climbs this would be the last chance for the race contenders to take time out of one another before the final time trial. After multiple attacks the second to last climb of the day, the Tourmalet, was descended. At the bottom, the lead group (with one rider several minutes ahead) was a strong one as it started up the Luz-Ardiden to finish the stage. As the group began the brutal climb among tightly packed fans along the route, Armstrong's handle bar caught an obstruction among the spectators, throwing him hard to the ground. Once back up and struggling to restart, his foot detached from his pedal, causing another delay. The lead riders, having moved ahead, slowed in order for the Texan to get back into the climb but much momentum had been lost. Almost immediately after the excitement, the group reformed and Spanish rider Iban Mayo attacked, opening a small gap. After over 100 miles of hard riding and having to remount after hitting the pavement, just finishing the stage would have been considered a victory. Following an attack at that point would seem to be impossible. However, Armstrong immediately jumped the gap to Mayo and, sensing an opportunity, attacked himself. No one else could keep his wheel as he pulled away. Maintaining a brutal pace on the steep climb he soon shredded all behind him, including his main rival Ullrich. Putting his game face on, Armstrong continued to hammer up the hill, soon catching the lead rider and heading for the finish. Sweat pouring off of him, he knew every second counted in this very close race. Picking up a time bonus as he won the stage, Armstrong showed who was still the boss as he gained time on all of his rivals, eventually securing his fifth TdF victory. It was said that this was what Henry Desgrange, the Tour founder, wanted when he added hills to the race route; suffering and victory no matter what the cost!

Mountain Domination

The 2004 Tour de France held great pressure for Lance Armstrong as he tried to become the first six-time winner of the event. While certainly dominant in mountain stages in the past it was as if he had made a conscious decision in the 2004 event to waste no opportunity as he completed the three week race. When the mountain stages appeared, the other riders certainly knew that the Texan was there to win. As the following accounts attest, Lance was giving away nothing that year.

Stage 12

As the 2004 Tour de France finally got to the real mountains (Pyrennes) Armstrong was over five minutes down in the general classification. After a flat first half the stage ended with two tough climbs. In a bunch near the lead at the base of the last climb, La Mongie, what was left of Armstrong's U.S. Postal team pulled the train, gradually wearing out the rest of the group. After his teammates dropped off, Lance responded to an attack, pulled even and then launched an attack himself. Only a few riders are able to stay with him as he headed for the finish. Attacking again Armstrong ended up on the wheel of the only one ahead of him, Italian Ivan Basso. The two pulled away and while certainly looking like he could have taken the stage win, Armstrong settled for second, picking up valuable time on everyone else. If it was a gift, it was certainly the last one of 2004.

Stage 13

The thirteenth stage of the 2004 TdF was the first true mountain stage of the race. After topping six climbs the U.S. Postal team train had reduced the peloton almost to ruins as only a small group was still in contention halfway through the final climb up the beyond category Plateau de Beille. Once the last of his teammates dropped off, the two strongest climbers in the 2004 race were once again going head to head. Working together this time, both Ivan Basso and Armstrong take turns leading up the severe, unrelenting slope through the mass of fans lining the roadway. Higher and higher they climbed through the human sea, each looking for the finish. With under a mile to go Armstrong zipped up his jersey; he would go for it today! With the line in site the Texan accelerated around Basso for the win.

Stage 15

After a transition ride toward the Alps for Stage 14, the peloton headed into the big mountains for Stage 15. While not containing any giant hills the route was packed with challenging climbs. At the base of the last climb the leading group is full of the usual suspects, including of course, Armstrong. The powerful group relentlessly moved up the hill, shredding riders along the way. As the finish line approached, four strong riders were left, those who would make up four of the top five places in the general classification at day's end. Ivan Basso made the first move but Armstrong, timing his attack to perfection, swung under the Italian around a corner to take the stage win, picking up the yellow jersey as the tour leader for the first time in the race.

Stage 16

The climb up L'Alpe d'Huez in the Alps is one of most difficult used in the Tour de France. In the 2004 version, one of the time trial stages was a battle up its slopes. In time trials, riders are all alone, forced to set tempo by themselves, as they start two minutes apart with their starting time determined by their place in the general classification (the last place rider goes first, the first place rider goes last..). Huge crowds lined the route, the largest of the race so far. Over the early phase of the ride Armstrong rode conservatively, and was in ninth place at the first time check. Picking up the pace in the middle of the race, Lance started to make up time, spinning his high cadence style up the slope. Soon another rider appeared in front of him, a target to acquire. It was Basso, his nemesis over the last week, who was getting caught, despite having started a full two minutes ahead! Armstrong pulled even and, not even glancing at his rival, accelerated around a corner and disappeared up the road. His face grim with determination, he continued to put time on every rider. As he crossed the finish line the stage, and the Tour, were all but over. Battling a mass of fans that parted only at the last minute as the riders passed, throwing water, encouragement, epithets and worse, Armstrong put in another amazing climbing performance, winning the stage and picking up additional minutes on all his rivals as he moved toward his record setting sixth TdF win. As Lance said afterwards, "I wanted it bad. I wanted it for the history on the mountain..."

Stage 17

With the GC lead and multiple stage wins at this point, conventional wisdom might have been to take it easy on the last mountain stage; to take no chances and cruise into Paris for the trophy. However, this was 2004 and something was in the air. A very tough day led over three category 1 and one beyond category climbs. The usual scenario played out as a strong group of five riders, including Armstrong, led over the top of the last big climb of the day. After a descent, the finishing stretch was rolling terrain with a slightly uphill finish. Armstrong's teammate, Floyd Landis, was in the lead group, and looking to pick up a stage win. With less than two kilometers to go Landis attacked but everyone went with him and soon he was reeled in. At the one kilometer to go mark the German rider Andreas Kloden suddenly took off from the back of the pack, surprising everyone and opening a big gap. It appeared the stage was his. As he saw Landis's hopes of winning fading away, Armstrong came out of the saddle and began to sprint. Pulling away from the others he amazingly closed the gap to Kloden in a flash and pulled past the German at the line, winning his third stage in a row. Winning four of five mountain stages (and finishing second in the fifth) Armstrong's performance in the 2004 TdF was one of the most dominating climbing exhibitions ever seen.

Top of the World

As previously mentioned, Mount Evans in Colorado is one of the most difficult climbs in the U.S. With the road soaring to over 14,000 feet, most of the difficulty is due to the altitude. The annual race up its slopes always draws many top climbers but by 2004 it had been twelve years since the course record had been assaulted. With snow having fallen the previous day and in cold and foggy conditions, American Tom Danielson put in a spectacular performance as he won the race by an unheard of 8 minutes and 40 seconds, chopping 4 minutes and 10 seconds off of the record. Having been training extensively at altitude and in mid-season form Danielson, one of the best climbers in the world (the current record holder on Mount Washington as of 2006 and multiple other climbs), raised the bar on Mount Evans and set a standard that may be difficult to surpass for some time to come.

The Lieutenant Strikes

Longtime faithful lieutenant to Lance Armstrong but a highly skilled rider in his own right, George Hincapie had never won a Tour de France stage despite numerous one day race wins. Stage 15 of the 2005 TdF was the most difficult of the race, containing four category 1 climbs and one beyond category climb to finish the stage. Getting into a breakaway early, Hincapie fought off many attacks as the stage progressed. Finally, on the last climb of the day, the Pla-d'Adet, Hincapie and Oscar Pereiro, who had done much of the leg work in the breakaway, pulled away from what was left of the leading group as the finish line approached. Marking Pereiro up the cruel steeps, Hincapie stayed behind while looking for the finish line. With 200 hundred meters to go he swung around the Spanish rider who had no response and charged to the hilltop win, becoming one of only a handful of Americans to win a major tour mountain stage.

A Tradition Continues

The 2006 Tour de France was considered wide open after the great one, Lance Armstrong, retired after his 7th straight win. American Floyd Landis came into that year's race well prepared. Having won several prestigious titles that year, he was poised to take over where Lance had left off. Leading the race as it headed into the Alps, Landis bonked on stage 16, losing his lead and much of his dignity in the process. Stage 17, he knew, might be his last chance at ever winning the Tour. It was a tough stage, with multiple difficult climbs along its route. Attacking early, the other riders sat back, thinking a move at this point was suicide. However, Landis knew just was he was doing. He quickly overtook an earlier breakaway group and continued hammering up the hills. Soon he was up by over nine minutes. What was left of the peloton finally woke up and began chasing in earnest. On the final climb of day, the beyond category Col de Joux Plane, Landis blew his last stage challenger off of his wheel and had a five minute lead at the summit. He then picked up an incredible additional 30 seconds on the field during the descent. Gaining over seven minutes on the overall leader that day, he went on to eventually win the TdF. Having attacked for over 80 miles through mountainous terrain, Landis's ride that day was one of the greatest in Tour history.

Map Legend

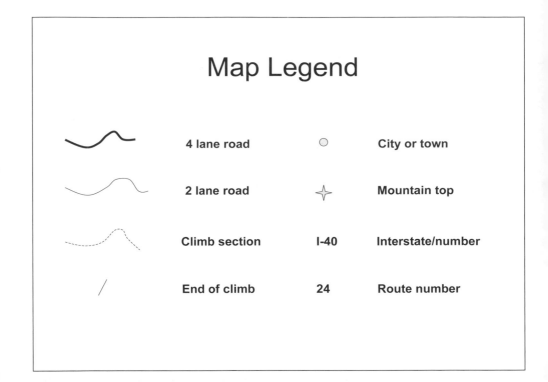

⌇	**4 lane road**	○	**City or town**
⌇	**2 lane road**	✦	**Mountain top**
⌇	**Climb section**	**I-40**	**Interstate/number**
/	**End of climb**	**24**	**Route number**

The start of the 13% grade final mile of California's Quimby Rd.

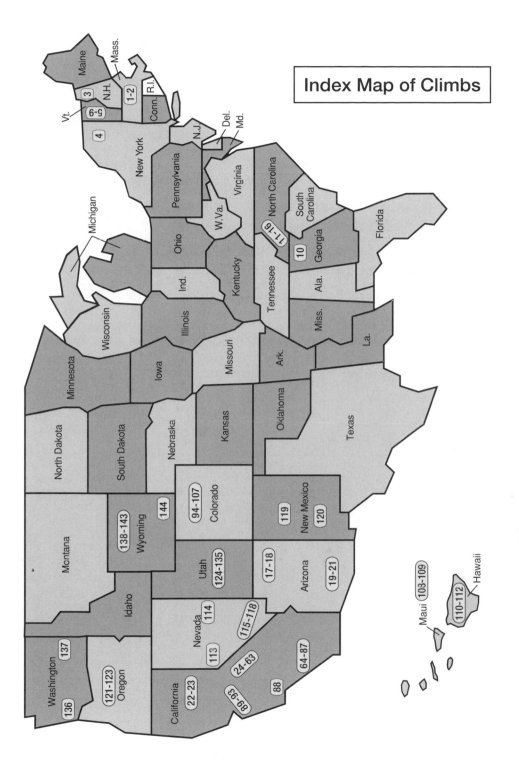

Index Map of Climbs

Northeast

Massachusetts

Mount Greylock (north)

Total elevation - 2,775 ft	Length - 7.7 miles
Average Grade - 6.8% (13%)	Rating - 1.93 (cat 1)

The northern approach to Mount Greylock is a stout and scenic climb. After 1.2 miles on Notch Rd turn left to enter the Mount Greylock State Reservation. At that point the road narrows and begins to twist and turn through deep woods, ending at a parking lot near the top of the mountain (closed in winter - Mt. Greylock State Reservation - 413 499-4262). A lot of top cyclists use this northeast gem for training. The south side of Greylock is quite a bit more tame although a scenic climb (9.6 miles at 4.5%).

Directions - In North Adams, MA head to the intersection of route 2 and Notch Rd where the climb begins by heading south on Notch Rd. Some list the start of this hill within Heritage Park in North Adams but while that does include a very steep starting stretch it also includes a significant flat section and results in an easier overall climb.

Facilities - North Adams, MA	**Airport** - Albany, NY

Kingsley Hill Road

Total elevation - 506 ft	Length - 0.5 miles
Average Grade - 19.2% (25%)	Rating - 0.97 (cat 2)

The first half mile of Kingsley Hill Rd is simply the steepest that I have found in the U.S. Don't blink in the small town of Monroe Bridge or you will miss the turnoff. The rough surface adds to the difficulty along with a significant stretch of 20+% grade. If you survive the first half mile keep going as the first mile of Kingsley Hill Rd is one of the steepest around (13.9%). The scenic road continues to climb after one mile but the worst (or best) is over at that point. The very steep road you see on the other side of the main road in Monroe Bridge (Monroe Hill Rd), while not nearly as steep, is also a tough climb.

Directions - In the tiny town of Monroe Bridge, MA head west on Kingsley Hill Rd from right in the center of town.

Facilities - North Adams, MA	**Airport** - Albany, NY

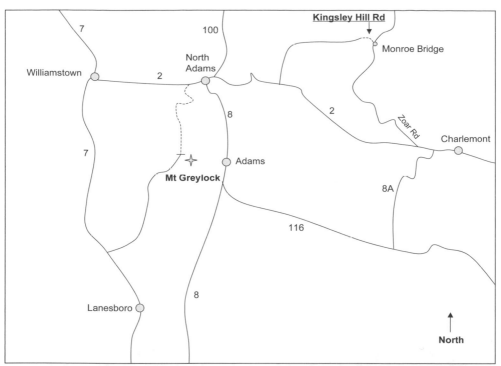

Mt. Greylock North and Kingsley Hill Rd, MA

Heading into deep woods on the north side of Mt. Greylock

New Hampshire

Mount Washington

Total elevation - 4,695 ft	Length - 7.5 miles
Average Grade - 11.9% (22%)	Rating - 6.45 (hors)

The most difficult road bike hill climb in the U.S. and perhaps the world, this road is only open to bikes during the annual hill climb race usually held in August and at times for several hours for a practice ride shortly before the race. No concession to gradient was made as it starts out steep and never lets up all the way to the top. Begin at the tollbooth where there is a brief shallow section and then the fun begins. A ramp of 12% grade smacks you in the face to let you know what is in store the rest of the way up the mountain. The grade eases slightly after 6/10ths mile but then soon kicks up with rolling ramps of 12-15% with occasional very short shallow sections to let you catch your breath (sort of). The trees soon begin to thin with some great views although it is difficult to appreciate them as you grind higher. Approximately 4 miles into the climb you round a bend and for the first time you see what is ahead of you (and it is not a pretty sight). At mile 4.4 the road turns to gravel for one mile (as of 2006, 21.3% of this road is not paved, however all of the unpaved sections of the road are easily ridden as the road receives so much traffic that the dirt/gravel is packed tight and smooth, and frequent rain eliminates dust much of the time. There are plans to eventually pave the entire climb) with sustained grades of 12-16% along a spectacular ridgeline. Several bends offer short relief before the torture resumes. The pavement returns but only for 1/10 mile at the 5,000 ft elevation marker. Another moderately steep section of gravel follows and then a very short (10-12 ft) section of pavement appears. After another 3/10ths mile of gravel the pavement returns for good. After a very steep turn to the left the grade then eases as you climb into a tundra-like setting. Rolling, slowly increasing grade leads you past the 6,000 ft elevation mark and at mile 7.4 a parking lot appears on the left. Just beyond the lot the steepest part of the climb greets you but the end is in site. The grade eases over the last few yards as you finish the climb at the brown souvenir hut. Mt. Washington is about the same length but considerably steeper than the famous Mortirolo in Italy and Angliru in Spain, generally considered among the hardest hill climbs used in European cycling tours (they are used sporadically in the Giro d'Italia and the Vuelta a Espana which are the national tours of Italy and Spain respectively). Mt Washington also has generally tougher weather to deal with compared to many other top climbs. If you ever get the chance to ride this hill, congratulate yourself on completing what may be the most difficult road bike climb on earth (closed in winter - Mt. Washington Auto Road - 603 466-3988 or www.mt-washington.com).

Directions - From Gorham, NH head south on route 16 for approximately 8 miles to Glen House. The Mt. Washington Auto Road is on your right. Head down the road 1/10 mile to begin the climb just beyond the toll booth.

Facilities - North Conway, NH	**Airport** - Manchester, NH

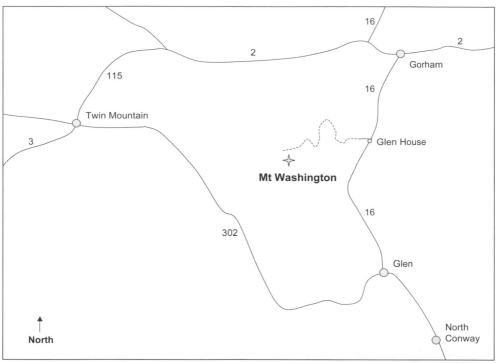

Mt. Washington, NH

Approaching the start of the vicious slopes of Mt. Washington

New York

Whiteface Mountain

Total elevation - 3,566 ft	Length - 7.9 miles
Average Grade - 8.6% (12%)	Rating - 3.13 (hors/cat 1)

Whiteface Mountain, which is closed to bikes until 5PM, is a very solid climb up to a castle-like visitor's center with restrooms. At the three mile mark you come to a toll booth. The grade is steep most of the way up and good views arrive near the top. This climb is almost identical in length and grade to the famous Tour de France climb of l'Alpe d'Huez, considered one of the most difficult used in that race. At the end of the road you can hike or take an elevator to the very top of the mountain. It is also one of the fastest descents in the U.S. and there is an annual race on its slopes (closed in winter - Whiteface Mountain Memorial Highway - 518 946-2223).

Directions - In Wilmington, NY the climb begins at the junction of routes 86 and 431 by heading up 431.

Facilities - Lake Placid, NY   **Airport** - Burlington, VT

The tollbooth about 3 miles up Whiteface Mountain

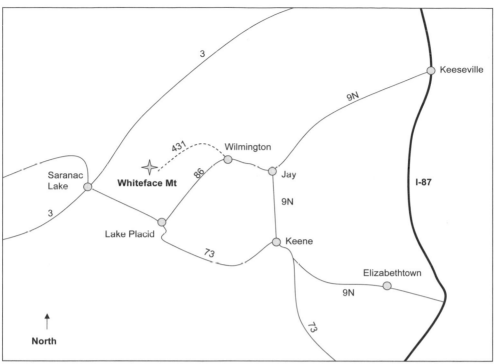

Whiteface Mountain, NY

Looking back at the top of the climb up Whiteface Mountain

Vermont

Lincoln Gap (east)

Total elevation - 1,098 ft	Length - 1.5 miles
Average Grade - 13.9% (21%)	Rating - 1.58 (cat 1/2)

This is a short but steep climb up the east side of Lincoln Gap (2,424 ft). From a shallow start at the beginning of the pavement the grade soon increases with the last mile averaging almost 16% which may be the most difficult paved mile of climbing in the U.S. Just before the summit the grade eases a bit. The entire route is through a thick tunnel of trees and is a must do ride for the serious hill climber. Head down the west side for a half mile (until the pavement ends) and then turn around to ride a section of 20% grade and one of the steepest half miles in the U.S. (closed in winter - Green Mountain National Forest - 802 767-4261). Make sure you are sufficiently warmed up for this one as you do not want to underestimate its fairly short length.

Directions - On route 100 just south of Warren, VT turn west on Lincoln Rd. Head west for 2.5 miles, going from pavement to gravel in the process. The climb begins where the pavement reappears.

Facilities - Montpelier, VT	**Airport** - Burlington, VT

Burke Mountain

Total elevation - 1,770 ft	Length - 2.5 miles
Average Grade - 13.4% (24%)	Rating - 2.47 (cat 1)

Burke Mountain is a very tough climb along an unrelenting grade in northern Vermont. Within the first mile (one of the steepest in the U.S.) there is extended 20% grade and the hill is steep all the way to the top. Often the average grade of this hill is overestimated which is understandable due to the extremely steep sections. At the parking area (mile 2.4) keep left and go around the gate to get to the very top of the pavement and another short section of 20% grade (closed in winter - East Burke Sports - 802 626-3215).

Directions - From the small town of East Burke, VT head east on route 114 for a short distance and turn right on Mountain Rd. Travel Mountain Rd for just over two miles and Campground Rd takes off from the left where the climb begins.

Facilities - East Burke, VT	**Airport** - Burlington, VT

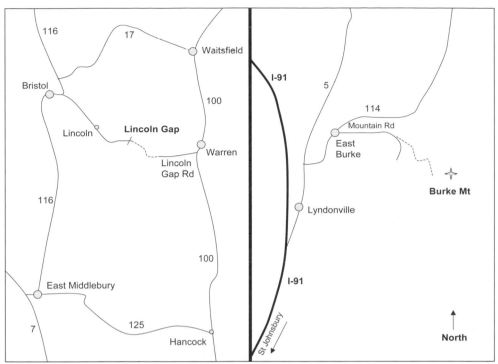

Lincoln Gap East and Burke Mountain, VT

The beginning of the steepest mile in the U.S. to Lincoln Gap

Mount Auscutney

Total elevation - 2,250 ft	Length - 3.7 miles
Average Grade - 11.5% (18%)	Rating - 2.74 (hors/cat 1)

Mount Auscutney is an extremely steep and difficult climb. There are extended ramps of 15% grade and except for a stretch near the top the entire climb is steep. The climb ends at a parking area near the top of the mountain. There is an annual race on its slopes (closed in winter - Mount Auscutney State Park - 802 674-2060; 800 299-3071 from Jan-April).

Directions - From the small town of Auscutney, VT head north on route 5. After several miles turn left on route 44A. The entrance to Auscutney State Park will appear on your left after 1.1 miles. Begin the climb at the toll booth ($2.50 per car/bike as of 2006).

Facilities - Lebanon, NH	Airport - Manchester, NH

Okemo Mountain

Total elevation - 2,190 ft	Length - 3.9 miles
Average Grade - 10.6% (17%)	Rating - 2.36 (cat 1)

This tough climb is through a ski area towards the top of Okemo Mtn. A steep mile in the middle of the route will test you. Toward the end the grade eases and the pavement ends.

Directions - In Ludlow, VT the climb begins at the junction of Okemo Mountain Rd and route 100 right in the middle of town.

Facilities - Ludlow, VT	Airport - Manchester, NH

Mount Equinox

Total elevation - 3,157 ft	Length - 5.2 miles
Average Grade - 11.5% (17%)	Rating - 3.79 (hors)

Mount Equinox is one of the most difficult climbs in the U.S. although it is open to bikes only during the Gear up for Lyme Race first held in 2004. Steep right from the start, there are multiple hairpin turns, one small descent and extended 13+% grade. At 4.2 miles the grade eases and the road travels along a ridge before one final steep section. The tollbooth is manned from 9AM - 8PM (closed in winter - Mt. Equinox Scenic Drive - 802 362-1114).

Directions - From Manchester, VT head south on route 7A for several miles. The Mt. Equinox toll road will be on your right.

Facilities - Manchester, VT	Airport - Albany, NY

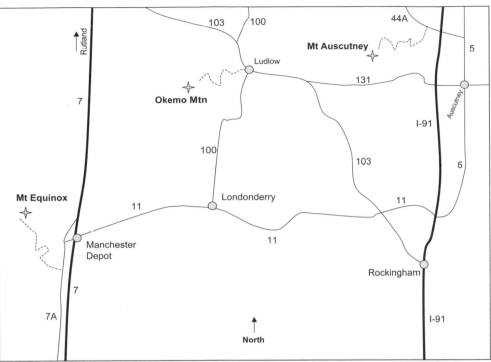

Mt. Auscutney, Okemo Mountain and Mt. Equinox, VT

The start of the very difficult climb up Mt. Equinox

Southeast

Georgia

Brasstown Bald

Total elevation - 1,824 ft	Length - 3.1 miles
Average Grade - 11.1% (20%)	Rating - 2.14 (cat 1)

This hill starts out steep along a very tight, twisty road with multiple ramps of 10-15% grade along with a section of 20%. The road comes to an apparent end after 2.5 miles at a parking area. From there you must ride the shuttle van road to the top, a half mile with an average grade of nearly 15% (bikes not allowed; the vans stop running at 6PM during summer). There is a national forest visitor's center on top (the highest point in Georgia) with great views of the surrounding mountains. If taken all the way up this is a tough hill. This climb is often used as a stage finish in the Tour of Georgia (closed in winter - Chattahoochee National Forest - 706 745-6928).

Directions - From Hiawassee, GA head south on route 17/75 for several miles to route 180. Turn right on route 180 and head 5.3 miles to 180 Spur on your right. The climb begins at the intersection of route 180 and 180 Spur.

Facilities - Helen, GA   **Airport** - Atlanta, GA

The beginning of the climb to Brasstown Bald

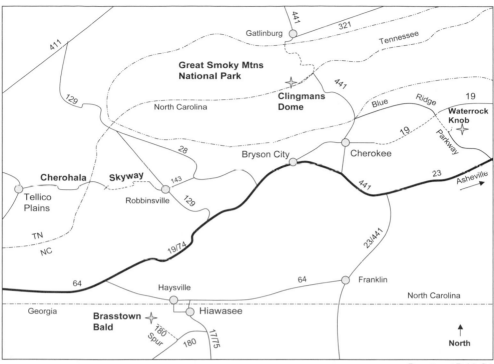

Brasstown Bald, GA

The start of the brutal final half mile of Brasstown Bald

45

North Carolina

19/Waterrock Knob

Total elevation - 3,771 ft   Length - 14.1 miles
Average Grade - 5.1% (10%)   Rating - 2.01 (cat 1)

Route 19 is a narrow road that carries some traffic. At mile 9.2 turn right onto the Blue Ridge Parkway and continue for 4.7 miles along a smooth surface before making a left turn for the short finishing climb to Waterrock Knob. There is a visitors' center with parking on top.

Directions - At the junction of routes 441 and 19 in Cherokee, NC turn north on 19. Head north past the casino and look for the bingo parlor on your right where you begin the climb.

Facilities - Sylva, NC   **Airport** - Asheville, NC

Cherohala Skyway (east)

Total elevation - 3,335 ft   Length - 11.6 miles
Average Grade - 5.5% (10%)   Rating - 1.87 (cat 1)

Cherohala Skyway is one of the most scenic and isolated climbs in the U.S. The top is reached after 11.5 miles (small parking area on the right - Huckleberry trailhead). After a descent the road continues to climb intermittently but without significant elevation gain.

Directions - In Robbinsville, NC go west on route 143. In 8/10ths mile turn left on Massey Branch Rd. Stay on Massey Branch for 3.4 miles and then turn right on 143 (Santeetlah Rd). Travel 4.5 miles to the corner of Santeetlah and Blue Boar Rd (right) to begin.

Facilities - Nantahala Outdoor Center, NC   **Airport** - Knoxville, TN

Clingmans Dome (west)

Total elevation - 4,826 ft   Length - 20.1 miles
Average Grade - 4.6% (8%)   Rating - 2.34 (cat 1)

Beginning in TN and ending in NC, ride through two short tunnels and make a unique 270 degree turn along the way. At Newfound Gap enter NC and turn right to Clingmans Dome (last 6.9 miles closed in winter - Great Smoky Mountains National Park - 865 436-1200).

Directions - In Gatlinburg, TN head east on route 441 for several miles, entering Great Smokey Mountains National Park. The climb begins at the visitor's center (on right).

Facilities - Pigeon Forge, TN   **Airport** - Knoxville, TN

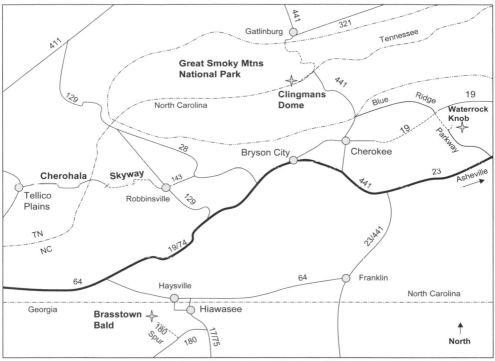

411
Gatlinburg
441
321
Tennessee

Great Smoky Mtns
National Park

129
North Carolina

Clingmans
Dome

441

Blue
Ridge
19

Waterrock
Knob

19

Parkway

28
Bryson City
Cherokee

Cherohala Skyway
143

23

Asheville

Tellico
Plains
Robbinsville
129

441

TN

NC

19/74

23/441

64
Haysville
64
Franklin

North Carolina

Georgia
Brasstown
Bald
Hiawasee

North

180
Spur
180
17/75

19/Waterrock Knob, Cherohala Skyway and Clingmans Dome West, NC

The beautiful scenery along Cherohala Skyway

Beech Mountain

Total elevation - 1,653 ft	Length - 3.5 miles
Average Grade - 8.9% (15%)	Rating - 1.56 (cat 1/2)

Beech Mountain is a difficult climb that was used as a stage finish in the now defunct Tour DuPont. Turn left on Ski Loft Rd at mile 3.1 to finish (4/10ths mile at 13%). Lance Armstrong used this hill early in his cycling recovery.

Directions - In Banner Elk, NC head west on 194 for 3/10ths mile to Beech Mountain Rd (on your right). The listed stats start from the dip 1/4 mile down Beech Mountain Rd.

Facilities - Banner Elk, NC	**Airport** - Tri-Cities, TN

Roan Mountain (north)

Total elevation - 3,097 ft	Length - 9.0 miles
Average Grade - 6.5% (10%)	Rating - 2.13 (cat 1)

This climb starts in Tennessee and is one of most difficult in the Southeast. The road switchbacks up the hill under a tunnel of trees with good views near the top. At mile 7.5 (Carvers Gap) enter North Carolina and turn right on Roan Mountain Rd for the final 1.5 miles. The south side of Roan Mountain is also a solid climb (10.9 miles at 5.4%)

Directions - From the small town of Roan Mountain, TN on route 19E head south on route 143. Travel 143 for 5.5 miles to begin the climb at Burbank Rd (on the left).

Facilities - Johnson City, TN	**Airport** - Tri-Cities, TN

Mount Mitchell

Total elevation - 5,161 ft	Length - 24.4 miles
Average Grade - 4.0% (10%)	Rating - 2.24 (cat 1)

This climb combines route 80, a section of the Blue Ridge Parkway and Mount Mitchell Rd. Climb route 80 up to the Blue Ridge Parkway. Turn left on the Parkway and ride through several tunnels (short). At mile 19.8 turn right on Mount Mitchell Rd to finish the climb on the highest paved road in the eastern U.S. (6,586 ft).

Directions - In Marion, NC, at the junction of routes 221 and 70, head south on 70. Go approx two miles and turn right on route 80. After 2.8 miles you come to the Lake Tohoma dam. Circle the lake to the small bridge over the creek that feeds the lake to begin the climb.

Facilities - Marion, NC	**Airport** - Asheville, NC

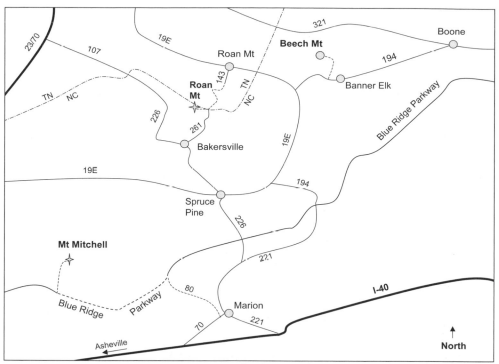

Beech Mountain, Roan Mountain North and Mt. Mitchell, NC

Great views from the north side of Roan Mountain

49

West

Arizona

Mincus Mountain (east)

Total elevation - 3,523 ft

Length - 13.3 miles

Average Grade - 5.0% (11%)

Rating - 1.93 (cat 1)

Mincus Mountain East is an interesting climb that travels through a restored mining town and into the high country of central Arizona. Soon after the climb begins you come to a 4-way stop sign. Continue straight ahead on Alternate 89. After several miles you enter the town of Jerome on an increasingly steep road. There is a short flat section then a ramp of 10%. At the stop sign in the middle of town turn right. The road then heads out of Jerome and into the mountains with great views down into the valley. After twisting up the side of a ridge and into big trees you enter Prescott National Forest. Soon you come to an elevation sign (7,023 ft) at an intersection. Turn right for 2/10ths mile to the hillcrest (the road continues but turns to dirt and descends). The other side of Mingus Mountain is a climb of ~2,000 ft over 11.9 miles from the town of Prescott Valley, AZ.

Directions - In Clarkdale, AZ take route 260 west to 11th Street (Old Highway 89A). Just south of Sunset St on the right the climb begins by heading up the hill toward the restored mining town of Jerome.

Facilities - Cottonwood, AZ

Airport - Phoenix, AZ

Humboldt Mountain

Total elevation - 1,646 ft

Length - 3.7 miles

Average Grade - 8.4% (12%)

Rating - 1.43 (cat 1/2)

Included due to its isolation and use in USCF races, Humboldt Mountain is a Sonoran desert climb on a narrow, poorly paved road. Other sources often list this hill as having an average grade of 11-12% which is inaccurate but it is still a challenging climb.

Directions - From Carefree, AZ (just north of Phoenix) head east on Cave Creek Rd. Continue straight on Cave Creek Rd at its junction with the road to Bartlett Reservoir. Soon after this the road becomes Forest Rd 24 and a bit further the pavement ends. After several miles of unpaved road the road to Humboldt Mountain appears on your right.

Facilities - Phoenix, AZ

Airport - Phoenix, AZ

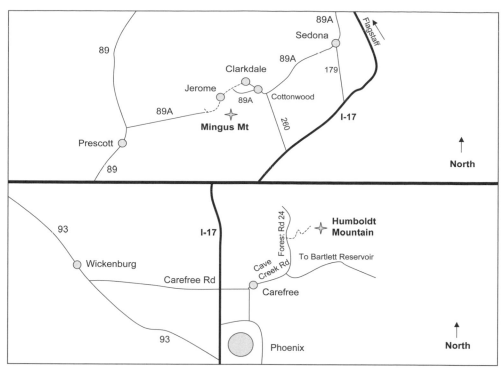

Mincus Mountain and Humboldt Mountain, AZ

The start of the climb up the east side of Mincus Mountain in AZ

Mount Graham

Total elevation - 5,572 ft	Length - 18.5 miles
Average Grade - 5.7% (11%)	Rating - 3.64 (hors)

Mount Graham is one of the top climbs in the U.S. After a straight start, the grade soon increases and you head through a serious of hairpin turns that is a classic section of road bike climbing. The listed climb ends at an unmarked top one half mile beyond mile marker 132 (road turns to the right). The road continues but consistent climbing has ended and the pavement ends after another 3.8 miles.

Directions - From Safford, AZ head south on route 666 for several miles to route 366 on your right. The climb begins at the intersection by heading west on route 366.

Facilities - Safford, AZ	Airport - Phoenix, AZ

Mount Lemmon

Total elevation - 6,222 ft	Length - 28.5 miles
Average Grade - 4.1% (10%)	Rating - 2.97 (hors/cat 1)

This is a long, classic climb out of the Sonoran desert. The road clings to the edge of the cliff in places making the bottom half very scenic. At mile 25.3 turn right on Ski Run Rd to continue. You soon pass through the ski area and continue on a single lane, poorly paved road. The climb ends at the locked gate. This road sees a lot of traffic on weekends.

Directions - In Tucson, AZ take Catalina Highway east. After the road goes from 4 to 2 lanes continue 4.2 miles to Mount Lemmon Short Rd on the right. The climb begins here.

Facilities - Tucson, AZ	Airport - Tucson, AZ

Kitt Peak

Total elevation - 3,579 ft	Length - 12.4 miles
Average Grade - 5.5% (10%)	Rating - 2.11 (cat 1)

This is a very isolated and scenic climb deep in the Sonoran desert. The road comes around the opposite side of the mountain towards the top with good views. At the Visitor's Center turn right up a single lane road to crest at one of the many telescopes on the mountain.

Directions - From Tucson, AZ head west on route 86 for approximately 35 miles. The Kitt Peak Observatory Road (Route 386) will be on your left and the climb begins at the junction.

Facilities - Tucson, AZ	Airport - Tucson, AZ

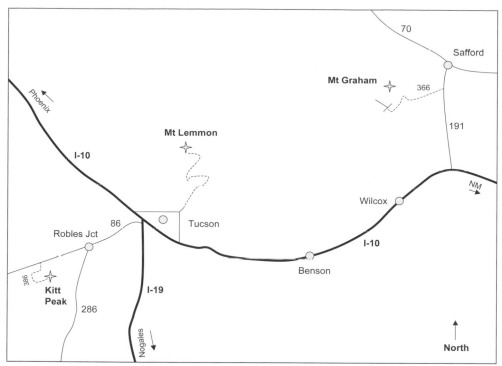

Mt. Graham, Mt. Lemmon and Kitt Peak, AZ

A scenic stretch heading up Mt. Lemmon

California

Mount Shasta

Total elevation - 4,326 ft	Length - 13.9 miles
Average Grade - 5.9% (11%)	Rating - 2.85 (hors/cat 1)

Mount Shasta is a scenic climb through the big trees of northern California. From the starting point, the road immediately begins to climb up the southwest flank of the mountain. After just less than a mile, turn left on Everett Memorial Hwy (A10). In several more miles you enter a pine forest which you glide in and out of all the way to the top. The climb is smooth and steady with no real steep pitches but the over 4,000 vertical feet of climbing make this a workout. The road opens up at the top into several small parking areas with great views. This hill is almost identical regarding length and grade to the Courcheval, a tough climb that is often used in the Tour de France (last 2 miles closed in winter - Shasta-Trinity National Forest - 530 926-4511).

Directions - From Mount Shasta, CA on I-5 exit to the right into town and then turn left on Mount Shasta Blvd. Go north on this road, just past the animal hospital, until you are almost out of town, and then turn right on Ski Village Rd. The climb begins at the intersection of Mount Shasta Blvd and Ski Village Rd.

Facilities - Mount Shasta, CA   **Airport** - Medford, OR

Lassen National Park (south)

Total elevation - 3,667 ft	Length - 15.8 miles
Average Grade - 4.4% (10%)	Rating - 1.83 (cat 1)

Listed primarily for its scenic qualities, this climb approaches Lassen Volcanic National Park from the south. The climb begins on route 89/36 at the intersection with route 72. Stay on 89 east as it immediately climbs out of a drainage through big trees. After 3.5 miles you reach Morgan Summit and turn right on 89 as you approach the park. The road climbs steadily as you near the Park entrance ($5 for bikes). It continues to climb within the Park on a narrow and twisty road. The views are spectacular but pay attention as there are big drop-offs as you near the summit (8,512 ft). The climb from the north is a less scenic and more shallow climb up to the pass (closed in winter - Lassen National Park - 530 595-4444).

Directions - In Red Bluff, CA on I-5 head east on route 36. Go 3.5 miles beyond the turn-off for the national park to the 2nd junction of routes 172 and 36 which is the starting point for this climb. You can also begin the climb in the small town of Mineral to the east of the junction of 36 and 89. The distance and elevation gain are nearly identical.

Facilities - Redding, CA   **Airport** - Medford, OR

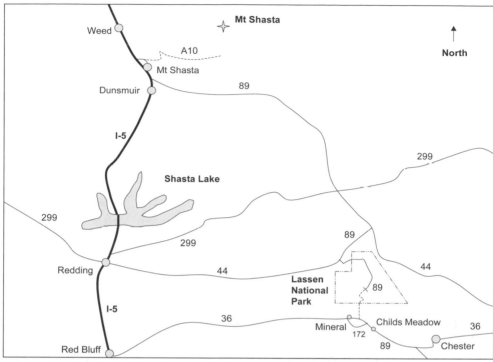

Mt. Shasta and Lassen National Park South, CA

Substituting is a massive switchback on super steep Iowa Hill Rd in California

55

Monitor Pass (east)

Total elevation - 3,216 ft	Length - 9.3 miles
Average Grade - 6.5% (11%)	Rating - 2.38 (cat 1)

This is a tough climb that rises out of the high desert near the Nevada border. A more difficult ascent than its western side, the grade is steady and eases off near the top to finish at 8,314 ft. Very hot in summer (closed in winter - Stanislaus National Forest 209 532-3671).

Directions - From Gardnerville, NV take 395 south for approximately 35 miles. The climb begins at the intersection of routes 89 and 395 by heading west on 89.

Facilities - Gardnerville, NV	**Airport** - Reno, NV

Monitor Pass (west)

Total elevation - 2,614 ft	Length - 7.9 miles
Average Grade - 6.3% (10%)	Rating - 1.85 (cat 1)

The west side of Monitor Pass is a solid and scenic climb along a creek. In the middle of the route the grade flattens near a small lake. Watch out for the two cattle guards on the descent (closed in winter - Stanislaus National Forest - 209 532-3671).

Directions - From Markleeville, CA head south on route 89 to its junction with route 4 where the climb begins by heading east up the hill on 89.

Facilities - Gardnerville, NV	**Airport** - Reno, NV

Sonora Pass (west)

Total elevation - 3,354 ft	Length - 9.1 miles
Average Grade - 7.0% (21%)	Rating - 2.86 (hors/cat 1)

This is a tough and scenic climb that heads east on route 108 through the rugged Sierras. The steepest section comes almost immediately and the first few miles are along double digit grade. The rest of the climb is variable with steep sections interspersed with several small descents. The final few miles ease a bit as you approach the summit but the entire route is very scenic. This is one of the great American climbs (closed in winter - Stanislaus National Forest -209 532-3671).

Directions - From Sonora, CA take 108 east for ~50 miles to Dardanelle. Several miles beyond, Kennedy Meadows Campground appears (right) where the climb begins.

Facilities - Sonora, CA	**Airport** - Sacramento, CA

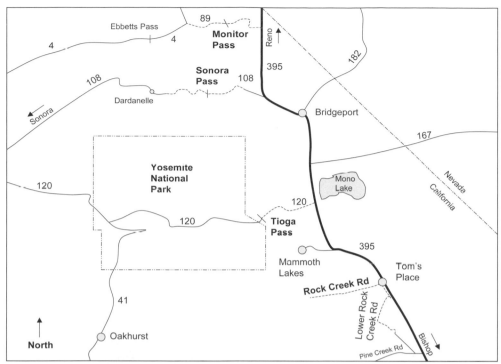

Monitor Pass East and West and Sonora Pass West, CA

The warning at the beginning of the west side of Sonora Pass

Sonora Pass (east)

Total elevation - 2,842 ft	Length - 9.4 miles
Average Grade - 5.7% (18%)	Rating - 2.02 (cat 1)

The east side of Sonora Pass is a very tough and scenic climb along a highly variable grade. The last seven miles average 7% and include multiple, double digit grade ramps along with a few small descents/flats. The final 3/4ths mile averages almost 14% (closed in winter - Stanislaus National Forest - 209 532-3671).

Directions - From Bridgeport, CA head north on route 395 for ~17 miles to route 108 on the left. Head west on route 108 for 5.2 miles to begin the climb where the grade increases.

Facilities - Gardnerville, NV   **Airport** - Reno, NV

Tioga Pass (east)

Total elevation - 3,175 ft	Length - 11.8 miles
Average Grade - 5.1% (9%)	Rating - 1.91 (cat 1)

This is a very dramatic climb on route 120 approaching Yosemite NP from the east. After about 4 miles the canyon opens up with spectacular views. The grade eases over the last two miles up to Tioga Pass at 9,945 ft (closed in winter - Yosemite NP - 209 372-0200).

Directions - From Bridgeport, CA take 395 south for ~25 miles to the junction of 120 (on the right) where the climb begins by heading toward Yosemite National Park.

Facilities - Mammoth Lakes, CA   **Airport** - Reno, NV

Rock Creek Road

Total elevation - 5,548 ft	Length - 20.5 miles
Average Grade - 5.1% (9%)	Rating - 3.38 (hors/cat 1)

Head up Lower Rock Creek Rd through one major descent to route 395. At the junction with 395 continue north for 9/10ths mile and turn left on Rock Creek Rd at Toms Place. Fairly shallow to start, the grade soon increases as you ascend. This route ends as the highest paved road in CA (10,220 ft) (closed in winter - Inyo National Forest - 760 876-6222).

Directions - From Bishop, CA head north on 395 for ~8 miles to its junction with Pine Creek Rd (left). Lower Rock Creek Road takes off on the right almost immediately. Follow this road 3.6 miles to the Inyo County line (Boundary Rd on left) where the climb begins.

Facilities - Bishop, CA   **Airport** - Reno, NV

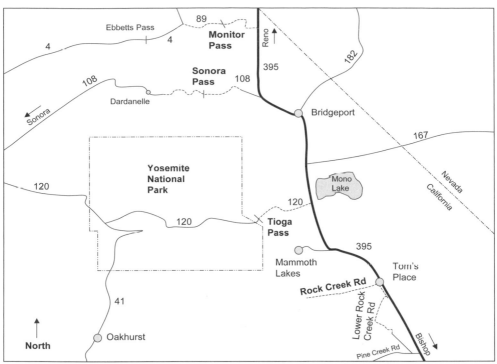

Sonora Pass East, Tioga Pass and Rock Creek Rd, CA

The scenic and spectacular climb to Tioga Pass

Pine Creek Road

Total elevation - 3,075 ft	Length - 8.7 miles
Average Grade - 6.7% (11%)	Rating - 2.29 (cat 1)

This is a stout climb along a creek within a steep-walled canyon. Like almost all climbs of the eastern Sierra, the grade increases as you ride. Very scenic in its upper end, the last 8/10ths mile is along a private, narrow road up to a mine.

Directions - From Bishop, CA head north on 395 for ~8 miles to its junction with Pine Creek Rd on the left. Head down Pine Creek Rd for 1.6 miles (school on left) to begin.

Facilities - Bishop, CA	**Airport** - Reno, NV

Lake Sabrina

Total elevation - 4,734 ft	Length - 15.6 miles
Average Grade - 5.8% (10%)	Rating - 3.15 (hors/cat 1)

Fairly shallow over the first two miles, the grade steadily increases up toward Lake Sabrina with big views down into the valley. After passing the South Lake junction the road heads toward a very spectacular alpine upper end; turning to one-lane before ending just above the lake at a small parking area (very top closed in winter - Inyo National Forest - 760 876-6222).

Directions – From route 395 in Bishop, CA take 168 (Line Rd) west for 3.2 miles to its intersection with Red Hill Rd (on the right) where the climb begins.

Facilities – Mammoth Lakes, CA	**Airport** – Reno, NV

South Lake

Total elevation - 5,445 ft	Length - 18.8 miles
Average Grade - 5.5% (14%)	Rating - 3.52 (hors/cat 1)

This climb shares its starting point and much of its length with Lake Sabrina. However, this one has a surprise in store toward the end. At mile 11.6 turn left toward South Lake. After a small dip and then several miles of shallow grade there are steep sections with grades running from 10-14% as you approach the top. The scenery is amazing however as the climb mercifully ends just above the stunning namesake lake at the end of the upper parking lot just shy of 10,000 ft (top section closed in winter - Inyo National Forest - 760 876-6222).

Directions - See Lake Sabrina above.

Facilities - Bishop, CA	**Airport** - Reno, NV

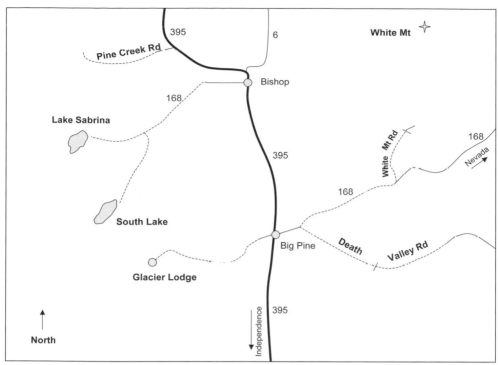

Pine Creek Rd, Lake Sabrina and South Lake, CA

Approaching the high Sierras on the climb to Lake Sabrina

Glacier Lodge Road

Total elevation - 3,747 ft	Length - 9.8 miles
Average Grade - 7.2% (12%)	Rating - 3.02 (hors/cat 1)

Glacier Lodge Road is a very difficult climb beginning in Big Pine, CA that leads into the high Sierras. It carries a steep grade almost all the way up to a scenic alpine setting (the lodge is no longer there). A big switchback approximately half way up will get your attention and the grade finally eases toward the top. The climb ends at a small parking area with great hiking possibilities. This is an extremely fast descent so watch the drop off into the creek and the cattle guard on the way down. This climb is almost identical in length and average grade to the mighty Tour de France climb of the Tourmalet (closed in winter - Inyo National Forest - 760 876-6222).

Directions - From route 395 in Big Pine, CA head west on Crocker St for 6/10th of a mile where the climb begins (unmarked beginning).

Facilities - Bishop, CA   **Airport** - Reno, NV

White Mountain

Total elevation - 6,204 ft	Length - 20.1 miles
Average Grade - 5.9% (11%)	Rating - 4.31 (hors)

This is a great ride and climb toward White Mountain out of massive Owens Valley. The first section is fairly shallow. Soon the grade increases and along a steep ramp the road passes through a unique one-lane section with blind corners. The grade then flattens out and you turn left on White Mountain Road at mile 12.7. After another somewhat shallow section the grade slowly increases and the road begins to roll up and down as you ascend. The last few miles are steep and at high elevation which may test some riders but the finishing stretch along a ridgeline offer great views of Owens Valley and the Sierras beyond. The hill crests at over 10,000 ft just before the pavement ends (closed in winter - Inyo National Forest - 760 876-6222). There is a seasonal visitor's center on top in the summer. A rough dirt road continues for quite a few miles to White Mountain. This is a long and tough climb so make sure you are prepared.

Directions - In Big Pine, CA head east on 168 for 2.2 miles to the junction with Death Valley Rd (on the right). The climb begins from there by continuing east on 168.

Facilities - Bishop, CA   **Airport** - Reno, NV

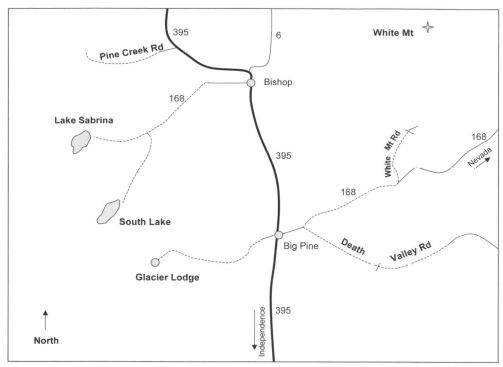

Glacier Lodge Rd and White Mountain, CA

The unique, one lane section heading up massive White Mountain

Death Valley Road (east)

Total elevation - 4,027 ft	Length - 14.0 miles
Average Grade - 5.5% (11%)	Rating - 2.43 (cat 1)

This isolated climb along Death Valley Rd is very interesting as it has steep ramps, good scenery and almost no traffic, ending at an unmarked but obvious summit. A very isolated beginning soon leads to the steepest section of climbing. The grade eases as you enter a valley. After several miles of fairly shallow climbing the grade increases again up to the unmarked but obvious pass at 7,670 ft. This is dry country so it can be climbed in most of winter and summer as well. Remember the isolated start however so carry anything you might need.

Directions - In Big Pine, CA head east on 168 for 2.2 miles to the junction of Death Valley, Rd on the right. Take Death Valley Rd over the pass and down into Eureka Valley. After 27.8 miles from the 168 junction the pavement changes and the road flattens into the valley. The climb begins here by turning around and riding west back the way you came.

Facilities - Bishop, CA	Airport - Reno, NV

Death Valley Road (west)

Total elevation - 3,722 ft	Length - 13.8 miles
Average Grade - 5.1% (9%)	Rating - 2.11 (cat 1)

The west side of Death Valley Rd is a solid climb with almost no traffic, ending at an unmarked pass. The first few miles are shallow and then the grade increases up the mountain. You break out with views near the top and the climb ends at an unmarked but obvious summit.

Directions - In Big Pine, CA head east on 168 for 2.2 miles to the junction of Death Valley Rd on the right where the climb begins.

Facilities - Bishop, CA	Airport - Reno, NV

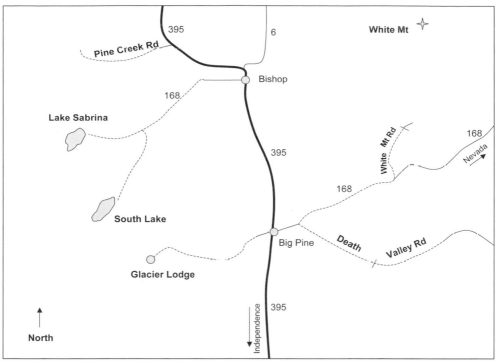

Death Valley Rd East and West, CA

The desolate beginning of the east side climb of Death Valley Rd

Onion Valley

Total elevation - 5,169 ft	Length - 12.5 miles
Average Grade - 7.8% (12%)	Rating - 4.68 (hors)

This is the hardest hill climb in California and one of the most difficult and spectacular in the world. Enjoy the first few miles as they are the only break you will get on this hill. As you ascend the grade continues to increase with the last ten miles averaging over 8%. The views of Owens Valley are amazing as you ride through multiple switchbacks over the last half of the climb. The climb ends at a parking area (the end is considered where the road splits at the beginning of the upper parking area) in an alpine bowl (9,163 ft). The descent is hair-raising. Onion Valley is significantly longer and almost as steep as Alp d'Huez, steeper and longer than the Tourmalet and the Galibier, and longer and as steep as the Madeleine, all famed French climbs that are regularly included in the Tour de France and considered the most difficult used in that Tour (closed in winter - Inyo National Forest - 760 876-6222).

Directions - From 395 in Independence, CA turn west on Market St. The climb starts 4/10ths mile down this road (which becomes Onion Valley Rd) at the cattleguard. Let the torture begin.

Facilities - Bishop, CA	**Airport** - Reno, NV

Whitney Portal

Total elevation - 4,580 ft	Length - 11.3 miles
Average Grade - 7.7% (13%)	Rating - 3.98 (hors)

Whitney Portal is a great and difficult climb out of the high desert up towards Mount Whitney, the highest mountain in the lower 48. Like most eastern Sierra ascents this one starts out tame and ends up tough. The grade increases as you climb so that the average grade over the last 5.5 miles is over 9%. The hill lets up just before the finish at Whitney Portal (8,371 ft) and a parking/hiking area (trailhead to Mt. Whitney). Whitney Portal is very similar to the famed French climb of the Madeleine, a monster frequently used in major cycling classics including regular appearances in the Tour de France (closed in winter - Inyo National Forest - 760 876-6222).

Directions - From highway 395 in Lone Pine, CA take Whitney Portal Rd west for 6/10ths mile to begin the climb where the road crosses the Los Angeles aqueduct.

Facilities - Bishop, CA	**Airport** - Reno, NV

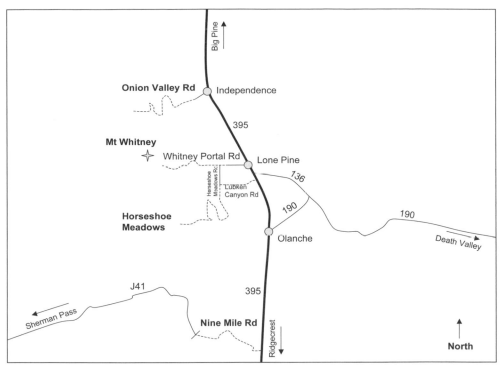

Onion Valley Rd and Whitney Portal, CA

A big switchback on rugged Mt. Whitney

Horseshoe Meadows

Total elevation - 6,234 ft	Length - 19.0 miles
Average Grade - 6.2% (12%)	Rating - 4.58 (hors)

Horseshoe Meadows is another very difficult eastern Sierra climb (look for the giant switchbacks on the flanks of the Sierras along route 395 just south of Lone Pine, CA). After 3.2 miles (which includes a very unique one lane road section through a horse pasture) turn left on Horseshoe Meadows Rd. A shallow section follows and then the road heads up the largest switchbacks the author has ever seen. This section is also the steepest but some of the best views on earth down into Owens Valley can help get you to the top. At mile 15.9 the road descends for 8/10ths mile and then resumes climbing. At mile 18.8 turn right toward the stables and pack station and the hill crests (unmarked) at just over 10,000 ft shortly thereafter. Be prepared before you tackle this one (closed in winter - Inyo National Forest - 760 876-6222).

Directions - At the junction of 395 and 136 just south of Lone Pine, CA head south on 395 for 2.6 miles to Lubken Canyon Rd on the right. Head west and the climb begins at the cattleguard a short distance up Lubken Canyon Rd.

Facilities - Bishop, CA	**Airport** - Reno, NV

Nine Mile Grade

Total elevation - 3,673 ft	Length - 9.9 miles
Average Grade - 7.0% (11%)	Rating - 2.75 (hors/cat 1)

Very similar in length and grade to the famed Tourmalet in France, Nine Mile Grade is a tough and little known climb up to Kennedy Meadows in the southern Sierras. From Highway 395 head west up Kennedy Meadows Rd. The first 1.5 miles are somewhat shallow but the grade soon gets and stays steep as the road enters the canyon. The route heads up the north side of the gorge with big drop-offs and great views. The hill crests at the Tulare County line. The road continues to Kennedy Meadows and can be used to reach Sherman Pass from the east, although it has descents with no sustained hill and is a long ride (closed in winter - Sequoia National Forest - 661 548-6503).

Directions - From Ridgecrest, CA take 395 north approximately sixteen miles to Kennedy Meadows Rd (on the left) where the climb begins.

Facilities - Ridgecrest, CA	**Airport** - Bakersfield, CA

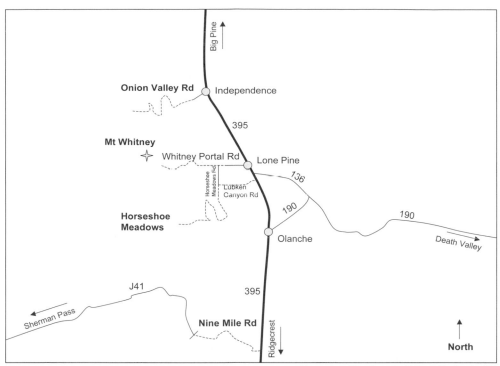

Horseshoe Meadows and Nine Mile Grade, CA

The very dramatic view heading up to Horseshoe Meadows

Wildrose

Total elevation - 4,455 ft	Length - 14.5 miles
Average Grade - 5.8% (10%)	Rating - 2.73 (cat 1)

Wildrose is one of the most isolated and unique climbs in the U.S. as portions of this route are no longer maintained. The first 5.5 miles are along a decent surface. You then enter Death Valley National Park and after that the surface resembles an old Pyrenees road as you must battle with debris and potholes. Near the top of Wildrose Rd you encounter three short, unpaved sections. At mile 9.5 turn right on the road to the Charcoal Kilns. The pavement here is a bit better (but not much) as you continue to climb within a valley. After a descent and final climb the hill ends where the pavement ends (the gravel road continues to Charcoal Kilns). Avoid this one in summer and carry an extra tube.

Directions - In Panamint Springs, CA head east on 190 for several miles to route 178 (road to Trona, CA). Head south on route 178 for ~14 miles to a stop sign. The climb begins here by heading left towards the mountains (turn right to reach Trona, CA).

Facilities - Ridgecrest, CA   **Airport** - Las Vegas, NV

Emigrant Pass (east)

Total elevation - 5,309 ft	Length - 21.8 miles
Average Grade - 4.6% (9%)	Rating - 2.54 (cat 1)

Emigrant Pass is a long climb that shares much of its length with the east side of Townes Pass as it heads out of Death Valley. From Stovepipe Wells head up route 190 within a very wide drainage and with dramatic mountain views. At mile 9.4 turn left on Wildrose Rd towards Emigrant Pass. This isolated section soon enters a narrow canyon and then a broad valley where the grade flattens. Near the end the grade gets steeper up to Emigrant Pass (5318 ft). The climb continues for another mile and ends at an unmarked top. Needless to say this one is a scorcher in the warmer half of the year.

Directions - In Death Valley National Park head to Stovepipe Wells to begin the climb by heading west on route 190.

Facilities - Ridgecrest, CA   **Airport** - Las Vegas, NV

Emigrant Pass (west)

Total elevation - 4,186 ft	Length - 15.5 miles
Average Grade - 5.1% (10%)	Rating - 2.23 (cat 1)

Emigrant Pass West follows the Wildrose climb to the stop sign at mile 9.5. Turn left (go

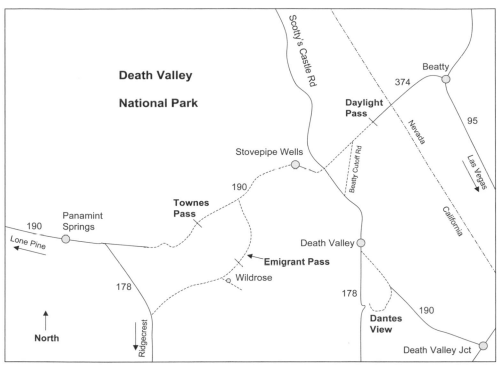

Death Valley

National Park

Scotty's Castle Rd

Beatty

374

Daylight
Pass

Nevada

95

Las Vegas

Stovepipe Wells

Beatty Cutoff Rd

190

**Townes
Pass**

Panamint
Springs

190

Lone Pine

Death Valley

Emigrant Pass

California

Wildrose

178

190

178

**Dantes
View**

North

Ridgecrest

Death Valley Jct

Wildrose, Emigrant Pass East and Emigrant Pass West, CA

A scene near the middle of the climb up Wildrose

right for the Wildrose climb) at the junction along old pavement. There is a steep switchback just before the finish and the climb ends at an unmarked summit (1.4 miles short of the signed Emigrant Pass). If you do not like heat, avoid this one in summer.

Directions - In Panamint Springs, CA head east on 190 for several miles to route 178 (road to Trona, CA). Head south on 178 for ~14 miles to a stop sign. The climb begins at this intersection by heading left towards the mountains (turn right to reach Trona, CA).

Facilities - Ridgecrest, CA   **Airport** - Las Vegas, NV

Townes Pass (east)

Total elevation - 4,759 ft	Length - 14.5 miles
Average Grade - 6.2% (9%)	Rating - 3.04 (hors/cat 1)

This is a tough climb out of Death Valley National Park. From Stovepipe Wells (sea level) the road heads up a huge alluvial fan, undulating as it goes with amazing views. The grade is never very steep but gradually increases all the way to just before the hill crests at Townes Pass (4,956 ft). The descent of this hill is a fast one. This side of Townes Pass is longer and steeper than the standard route up the Col du Glandon, a difficult climb often used in the TdF. Avoid this one in summer.

Directions - In Death Valley National Park head to Stovepipe Wells. Travel 2.4 miles west on route 190 to begin the climb.

Facilities - Ridgecrest, CA   **Airport** - Las Vegas, NV

Townes Pass (west)

Total elevation - 3,406 ft	Length - 9.4 miles
Average Grade - 6.9% (11%)	Rating - 2.40 (cat 1)

The west side of Townes Pass is a tough desert climb that leads out of isolated Panamint Valley and into Death Valley. From the valley floor the road eventually heads up a drainage. The first two miles are shallow but then you must negotiate a very tough five mile stretch of over 8% grade. The final few miles ease back to finish at signed Townes Pass (4,956 ft). The west side of Townes Pass is more difficult than the Col d'Aspin and La Mongie, and quite similar to Luz-Ardiden; all difficult climbs that make regular appearances in the Tour de France.

Directions - From Panamint Springs, CA head east on 190 (toward Death Valley). The climb begins where 190 starts to climb out of the valley (the listed stats begin where the sand ends).

Facilities - Ridgecrest, CA   **Airport** - Las Vegas, NV

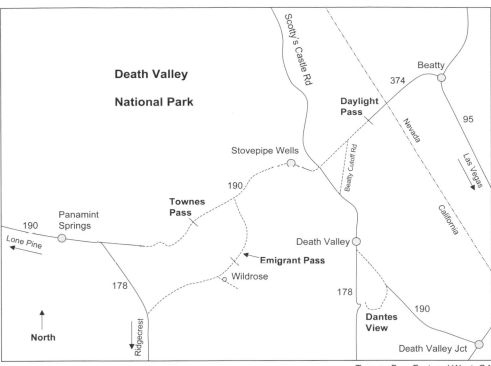

Death Valley

National Park

Scotty's Castle Rd

Beatty

374

Daylight
Pass

95

Nevada

Las Vegas

Stovepipe Wells

Beatty Cutoff Rd

190

Townes
Pass

Panamint
Springs

190

Lone Pine

California

Death Valley

Emigrant Pass

Wildrose

178

178

190

North

Ridgecrest

Dantes
View

Death Valley Jct

Townes Pass East and West, CA

6% GRADE
5 MILES

Looking down into Death Valley along the climb to Townes Pass

Daylight Pass

Total elevation - 4,382 ft	Length - 14.3 miles
Average Grade - 5.8% (10%)	Rating - 2.60 (cat 1)

Head east on route190 from Sand Dunes Rd for one mile then turn left on Scottys Castle Rd. After a half mile turn right toward Beatty, NV on Daylight Pass Rd. After passing the junction with the Beatty Cut-off Rd the grade increases to finish at Daylight Pass (4317 ft).

Directions - From Stovepipe Wells in Death Valley National Park head east on 190 to Sand Dunes Rd (dirt road on the left) where the climb begins by continuing east on 190.

Facilities - Ridgecrest, CA   Airport - Las Vegas, NV

Daylight Pass Long

Total elevation - 4,483	Length - 15.8 miles
Average Grade - 5.4% (10%)	Rating - 2.47 (cat 1)

This route up to Daylight Pass is a solid climb with the lowest beginning elevation of any US climb (166 ft below sea level). You reach a junction at mile 9.9 and then keep right up to the pass within a canyon. This finishing section is steeper (average grade 6.5%) than the lower section.

Directions - From the Furnace Creek Visitors Center in Death Valley National Park head north on 190 for ~11 miles to the Beatty Cutoff road on your right where the climb begins.

Facilities - Ridgecrest, CA   Airport - Las Vegas, NV

Dantes View

Total elevation - 5,475 ft	Length - 23.6 miles
Average Grade - 4.4% (14%)	Rating - 2.50 (cat 1)

This is long climb from sea level that heads up route 190 for 10.6 miles and then turns right on the road to Dantes View. Fairly shallow much of the way, the grade increases toward the top and includes a ramp of 12% within the last quarter mile. The climb finishes (5,475 ft) at a parking area with one of the best views around. The author rode this hill on a cool November day with temps around 85 degrees so summer is an oven.

Directions - From the Death Valley NP Visitors Center head east on 190 to its junction with 178 (the road to Bad Water). The climb begins at the junction by continuing east on 190.

Facilities - Las Vegas, NV   Airport - Las Vegas, NV

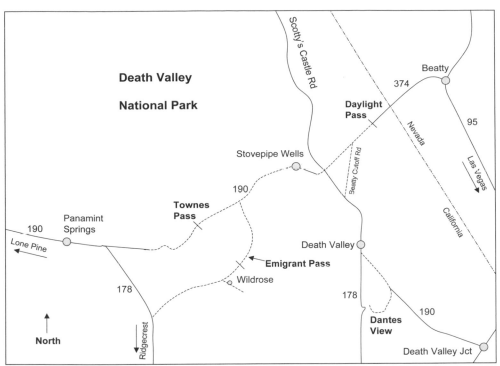

Dantes View, Daylight Pass and Daylight Pass Long, CA

Looking down into Death Valley along Daylight Pass Long

Old Priest Grade

| Total elevation - 1,522 ft | Length - 2.2 miles |
| Average Grade - 13.1% (19%) | Rating - 2.06 (cat 1) |

One of the steepest roads in the U.S., Old Priest Grade is a classic climb. It includes one of the most difficult miles in the country and is steep from bottom to top. Once you turn onto Old Priest Grade Rd (0.3 miles) make sure you are ready to climb as the next half mile is the steepest on the hill and one of the steepest in the country. This road is very narrow with guardrails and several blind corners so be alert at all times. The climb ends at route 120, another very pleasant ascent and a better descent (much safer than the dangerous Old Priest Grade). This a great place to climb and descend although both roads carry some traffic.

Directions - From the junction of routes 49 and 120 south of Chinese Camp, CA, head east on 120 (toward Yosemite National Park) for 7/10ths mile to Old Priest Grade Rd on the right. At that junction, turn right and then immediately turn right again on Moccasin Switchback Dr and descend 3/10ths mile to Lake Shore Drive (near the dam). The climb starts here by retracing your route on Moccasin Switchback Dr and turning right on Old Priest Grade Rd to continue the climb.

| Facilities - Sonora, CA | Airport - Oakland, CA |

Cold Springs Summit

| Total elevation - 3,756 ft | Length - 11.5 miles |
| Average Grade - 6.2% (10%) | Rating - 2.55 (cat 1) |

Cold Springs Summit is reached via Beasore Rd very close to Bass Lake. It climbs through a thick forest along a very solid grade, ending at the signed summit (7308 ft). The grade is very consistent all the way up the hill. It is a scenic climb as well with moss covered pine trees near the top. You can continue riding after the pass along a scenic road. There is very good mountain biking in the area as well.

Directions - In Oakhurst, CA head north on route 41 for several miles and turn right on Bass Lake Rd. From there travel for several miles until Bass Lake comes into view on the right. Beasore Rd will appear after a short distance on your left which takes you up to Cold Springs Summit.

| Facilities - Fresno, CA | Airport - Fresno, CA |

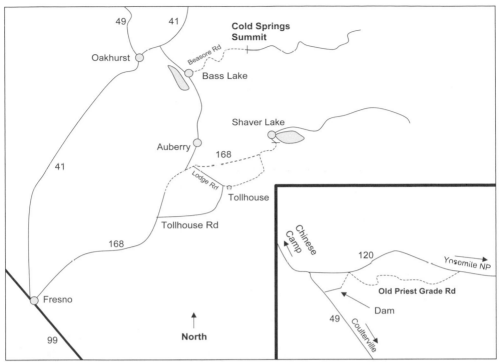

Old Priest Grade and Cold Springs Summit, CA

The incredibly steep Old Priest Grade

77

Tollhouse Road/168

Total elevation - 3,630 ft	Length - 9.8 miles
Average Grade - 7.0% (11%)	Rating - 2.63 (cat 1)

This climb is steep immediately as the road heads through town and then up a ridge with good views. A variable grade makes this one a bit tougher than its statistics suggest. At mile 7.4 you intersect with highway 168. Turn right on 168 and head up the hill. The road soon enters the trees and narrows. After just over three miles on 168 the hill crests at Littlefield Rd on the right just before the small town of Shaver Lake. This is one of the most difficult ten mile stretches of climbing in the U.S.

Directions - From Fresno, CA take 168 east to the small community of Academy. Continue east another six miles to Tollhouse Rd on the right. Head east up Tollhouse Rd from its intersection with route 168 for ~8.5 miles to its junction with Lodge Rd (left). This previous section is a pleasant ride and does gain in elevation but it is too shallow to include as part of the hill climb. At the Lodge Rd junction you turn right to stay on Tollhouse Rd. After another 8/10ths mile the climb begins at a bridge over a small creek just as you enter the small town of Tollhouse.

Facilities - Fresno, CA   **Airport** - Fresno, CA

168

Total elevation - 4,688 ft	Length - 16.2 miles
Average Grade - 5.5% (10%)	Rating - 2.68 (cat 1)

168 is a tough climb up into the Sierras that shares its finish with the previous climb. At five miles the road becomes four lane and the grade from this point forward becomes quite consistent. This route carries much more traffic than Tollhouse Rd (previous climb). At mile thirteen it reduces back to two lanes. The hill crests at Littlefield Rd on the right just before the small town of Shaver Lake. You can really fly for much of the descent but be careful of the right hand turn at the junction soon after the road reduces back to 2 lanes as you descend.

Directions - From Fresno, CA head east on 168 for ~20 miles to Gooseberry Rd on the right where the climb begins. 168 begins to climb before this listed start but with multiple flats/descents.

Facilities - Fresno, CA   **Airport** - Fresno, CA

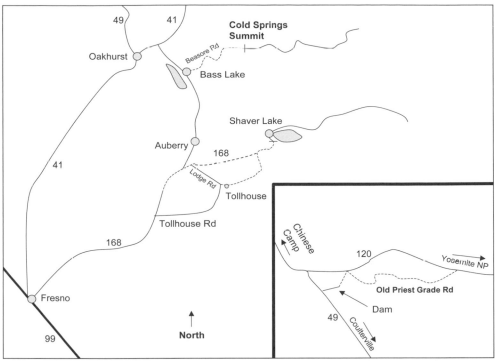

Tollhouse Rd/168 and 168, CA

A scene near the bottom of the climb up Tollhouse Rd/168

180 (west)

Total elevation - 5,163 ft	Length - 20.2 miles
Average Grade - 4.8% (9%)	Rating - 2.68 (cat 1)

This is a long climb east of Fresno, CA that leads into Kings Canyon National Park. Good views and big trees near the top help ease the pain of a long climb. After ~19 miles you pass through the park entrance gate ($5 for bikes) and the hill crests soon after at a junction.

Directions - From Fresno, CA take 180 east to the small town of Squaw Valley. The climb begins just east of town at the bridge over Mill Creek.

Facilities - Fresno, CA	Airport - Fresno, CA

Kings Canyon

Total elevation - 3,390 ft	Length - 11.0 miles
Average Grade - 5.8% (10%)	Rating - 2.14 (cat 1)

This is a very scenic climb out of Kings Canyon. A steady grade all the way up is softened by great views and big trees near the top. The hill crests at an unmarked summit near McGee Point (closed in winter – Sequoia & Kings Canyon NP - 559 565-3730).

Directions - Within Kings Canyon NP take route 180 down into the park to the Kings River. Turn around and travel 5 miles to begin the climb where the road makes a 90 degree turn up Tenmile Creek (climb back up toward the park entrance).

Facilities - Fresno, CA	Airport - Fresno, CA

J21/245/180

Total elevation - 5,750 ft	Length - 25.3 miles
Average Grade - 4.3% (10%)	Rating - 2.66 (cat 1)

This is a long climb up the slopes of the Sierras into Sequoia country. After nine miles on J21 (single lane in places) turn right on 245. 245 is a busier road that twists up the hillside with a few short descents. Turn right at the intersection with 180 and continue on a very scenic stretch of road into the National Park ($5). The climb ends soon after at a junction.

Directions - From Visalia, CA head east on 198 to Lemon Cove, CA. In Lemon Cove, turn left on route 216 and then a quick right on Dry Creek Rd (J21). Head up J21 for about 8.5 miles to the bridge over the creek where the climb begins.

Facilities - Visalia, CA	Airport - Fresno, CA

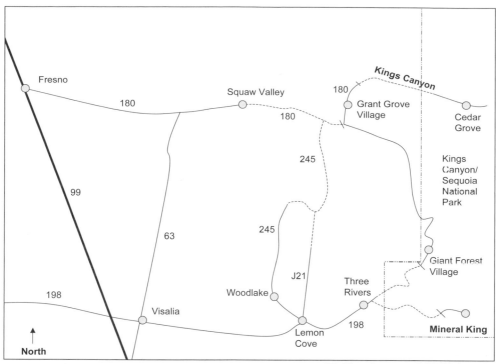

Fresno

Squaw Valley

Kings Canyon

180

180

180

Grant Grove
Village

Cedar
Grove

245

Kings
Canyon/
Sequoia
National
Park

99

63

245

Giant Forest
Village

J21

Three
Rivers

Woodlake

Visalia

198

198

Lemon
Cove

Mineral King

↑
North

180, Kings Canyon and J21/245/180, CA

The mighty Kings River Gorge

Total elevation - 4,711 ft	Length - 20.3 miles
Average Grade - 4.4% (10%)	Rating - 2.22 (cat 1)

This is a fairly long and scenic climb from the Sierra foothills up into large redwoods. Turn right at the intersection with 180 and continue on a scenic stretch of road into Kings Canyon NP ($5). The climb ends at the junction of the road to Sequoia National Park.

Directions - From the small town of Woodlake, CA head north on route 245. After ~12 miles Boyd Dr appears on the left. After another 6.6 rolling miles the grade increases as the road make a 90 degree turn to the right where the listed climb begins.

Facilities - Visalia, CA	**Airport** - Fresno, CA

Sequoia

Total elevation - 5,120 ft	Length - 16.6 miles
Average Grade - 5.8% (11%)	Rating - 3.19 (hors/cat 1)

Sequoia is a classic climb with amazing views. After a half mile you pass the Sequoia NP entrance station ($5 for bikes). The road then continues twisting up the ridge through multiple switchbacks, generally increasing in grade as you climb. Giant Sequoias appear near the top. The climb ends at the intersection with Morro Rock Rd on the right. Sequoia is significantly longer and as steep as the famous TdF climb of the Col d'Izoard.

Directions - From Visalia, CA head east on 198 through the town of Three Rivers. The climb begins at the bridge where 198 crosses the Kaweah River just beyond Three Rivers.

Facilities - Visalia, CA	**Airport** - Fresno, CA

Mineral King Road

Total Elevation - 4,812 ft	Length - 17.5 miles
Average Grade - 5.2% (12%)	Rating - 2.63 (cat 1)

A very twisty and scenic climb up into the high country along one of the most narrow two lane roads around. The climb ends where the pavement ends. Statistics are estimated (closed in winter - Sequoia & Kings Canyon National Park - 559 565-3730).

Directions - From Visalia, CA head east on 198 through the town of Three Rivers. Mineral King Rd will be on the right as you exit town. The climb begins at the junction.

Facilities - Visalia, CA	**Airport** - Fresno, CA

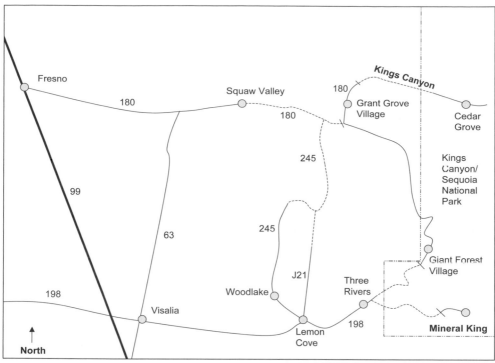

245/180, Sequoia and Mineral King Rd, CA

A scene about halfway up the climb to Sequoia

Total elevation - 6,199 ft	Length - 24.0 miles
Average Grade - 4.9% (9%)	Rating - 3.32 (hors/cat 1)

This is a long, solid climb that starts just east of Springville, CA. From the bridge over the North Fork of the Tule River, head up the hill along a drainage. Great views of the drainage down low and thick trees up top make this a scenic climb. The grade is steady all the way up this very long hill. The climb crests a half mile beyond Quaking Aspen at the junction with the road to Needles Springs (dirt) on the left (closed in winter - Sequoia National Forest - 661 548-6503).

Directions - From the small town of Springville, CA head east on route 190 to the bridge over the North Fork of the Tule River where the climb begins.

Facilities - Visalia, CA	**Airport** - Bakersfield, CA

Parker Pass (west)

Total elevation - 2,883 ft	Length - 8.7 miles
Average Grade - 6.3% (10%)	Rating - 1.93 (cat 1)

The west side of Parker Pass is a scenic and difficult climb that ends after 8.7 miles at an unmarked top. You can continue 1.3 miles further down the road to its junction with the Great Western Highway. The east side of Parker Pass is also scenic but a more shallow climb up from the Kern River (closed in winter - Sequoia National Forest - 661 548-6503).

Directions - From the small town of California Hot Springs on J-22/Hot Springs Rd continue east toward Johnsondale. 3.3 miles from California Hot Springs you cross a creek after a descent. The climb begins here.

Facilities - Kernville, CA	**Airport** - Bakersfield, CA

Shirley Meadows (east)

Total elevation - 4,105 ft	Length - 9.9 miles
Average Grade - 7.9% (19%)	Rating - 3.57 (hors)

The east side of Shirley Meadows along route 155 is a very tough climb along a highly variable grade that ends at a ski area. It includes the most difficult five-mile stretch of climbing west of the Mississippi along multiple double-digit grade ramps so go prepared. At mile 7.5 turn left on Rancheria Rd where the grade eases a bit. The climb ends at the Shirley

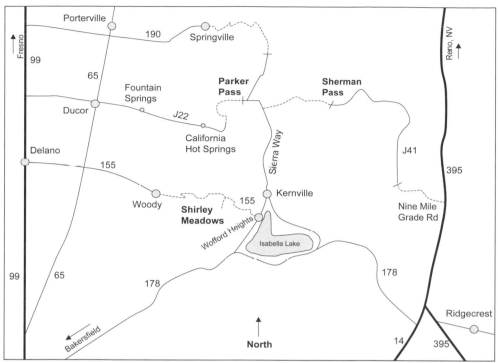

190, Parker Pass West and Shirley Meadows East, CA

A steep section along the very difficult east side of Shirley Meadows

Meadows ski area parking lot. This side of Shirley Meadows is longer and almost as steep as l'Alp d'Huez and steeper and almost as long as the Tourmalet, two of the most famous and difficult climbs used regularly in the Tour de France. It is a tough descent so watch the multiple blind curves heading down.

Directions - From Wofford Heights, CA begin the climb where route 155 takes a 90 degree turn up the hill to the west.

Facilities - Kernville, CA   **Airport** - Bakersfield, CA

Shirley Meadows (west)

Total elevation - 5,133 ft	Length - 24.5 miles
Average Grade - 4.0% (11%)	Rating - 2.20 (cat 1)

This is a long, twisty climb up to a ski resort. Never very steep and with some small descents, it does provide a good workout due to its length. It is exposed over much of its course with consistent shade only near the top. After 22.1 miles turn right on Rancheria Rd to finish at the Shirley Meadows Ski area parking lot.

Directions - The climb begins by heading east on 155 from the small town of Woody, CA.

Facilities - Bakersfield, CA   **Airport** - Bakersfield, CA

Sherman Pass (west)

Total elevation - 5,316 ft	Length - 15.2 miles
Average Grade - 6.6% (10%)	Rating - 4.06 (hors)

The west side of Sherman Pass is one of the toughest climbs in this guide. Isolated, beginning at the Kern River, the road immediately heads up the drainage at a steady grade. Be prepared as this hill will test you through multiple switchbacks ending shy of the actual pass at 9126 ft (just beyond the cattleguard). Desert-like at the bottom, you ride through big trees near the top. Sherman Pass is longer and almost as steep as Mt Ventoux, perhaps the most difficult climb in France (closed in winter - Sequoia National Forest - 661 548-6503). There is no sustained climb from the east side of the pass.

Directions - From Kernville, CA head north along the Kern River on Sierra Way for ~18 miles to its junction with Sherman Pass Rd (on the right) where the climb begins.

Facilities - Kernville, CA   **Airport** - Bakersfield, CA

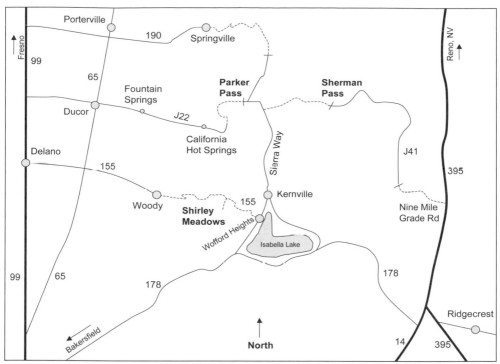

Shirley Meadows West and Sherman Pass, CA

Descending near the top of Sherman Pass

S22

Total Elevation - 3,520 ft	Length - 12.1 miles
Average Grade - 5.5% (9%)	Rating - 1.98 (cat 1)

S22 is a solid climb out of the low desert of Anza-Borrego Desert State Park. It ends at an unmarked summit as the grade flattens out on top. It is a scorcher in summer.

Directions - From the town square in Borrego Springs, CA head west on S22 for 1.3 miles. The climb begins at that point where S22 makes a left turn and heads up the hill.

Facilities - Borrego Springs, CA   **Airport** - San Diego, CA

Palomar Mountain

Total elevation - 4,735 ft	Length - 13.2 miles
Average Grade - 6.8% (14%)	Rating - 3.43 (hors)

Palomar Mountain is a very difficult climb, along with Mount Baldy the toughest in Southern California. From tiny Pauma Valley head up the hill on route 76. After ~ 6 miles turn left on S6 (toward Palomar) and you soon begin to switchback up the hill on an increased grade. At the stop sign turn right on S7 then in 1/10 mile go left on Crestline Rd. In a half mile turn left up to Palomar Mountain County Park for a short, steep finish. This climb is longer and as steep as the standard route up the Galibier, a regular beyond category Tour de France climb.

Directions - Begin the climb in the small town of Pauma Valley, CA (north end) on route 76. You can also begin the climb on S6 one mile south of the small town of Rincon (just beyond Harrah's Casino).

Facilities - Escondido, CA   **Airport** - San Diego, CA

74 (east)

Total elevation - 4,734 ft	Length - 22.7 miles
Average Grade - 4.0% (9%)	Rating - 1.92 (cat 1)

74 is a very long and scenic desert climb with a steady grade. Near the top the climb has some small ups and downs before ending at the Santa Rosa Summit (just before the Pacific Crest Trail crosses route 74). This can be a great winter climb but is very hot in summer.

Directions - In Palm Desert, CA head to the corner of route 74 and El Passeo where the climb begins by heading west on 74.

Facilities - Palm Springs, CA   **Airport** - Palm Springs, CA

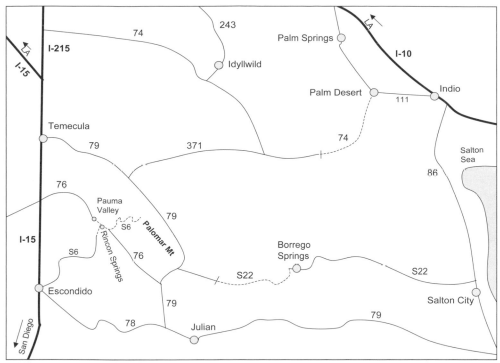

S22, Palomar Mountain and 74 West, CA

A scene near the top of Palomar Mountain

Valley of the Falls

Total elevation - 4,279 ft	Length - 14.5 miles
Average Grade - 5.6% (13%)	Rating - 2.53 (cat 1)

Head up the hill out of town towards Big Bear along route 38 which does carry some traffic. After passing Bryant St on your right you soon enter a gorge. At mile 10.3 turn right on Valley of the Falls Rd. The traffic deceases and the grade and quality of scenery increase as you head into the canyon. Trees and a small community soon appear along with short ramps of 10-13% between small descents. Ride the road until it ends at a parking area for the national forest.

Directions - In Mentone, CA head east on route 38 to the last stoplight which is Crafton Street. The climb begins here by continuing east on 38.

Facilities - San Bernardino, CA   **Airport** - Palm Springs, CA

Angeles Oaks

Total elevation - 4,032 ft	Length - 15.3 miles
Average Grade - 5.0% (9%)	Rating - 2.11 (cat 1)

This climb shares much of its length with Valley of the Falls climb (previous). Keep straight at the Valley of the Falls turnoff (stay on route 38). The road soon begins to twist up the hill along a classic section of climbing with good views within the San Bernardino Mountains. Eventually you reach the small town of Angeles Oaks, CA where the climb ends at the fire station.

Directions - This climb shares it's beginning with Valley of the Falls (see previous climb) beginning in Mentone, CA.

Facilities - San Bernardino, CA   **Airport** - Palm Springs, CA

330

Total elevation - 4,588 ft	Length - 14.2 miles
Average Grade - 6.1% (10%)	Rating - 2.97 (hors/cat 1)

330 is a surprisingly tough climb up into the San Bernardino Mountains north and east of Los Angeles. This twisty road carries some traffic and there are some narrow sections with big drop offs, particularly over the bottom section. The grade over the first half of the climb is deceptive and you will work to get over it. Good views appear near the top and the grade

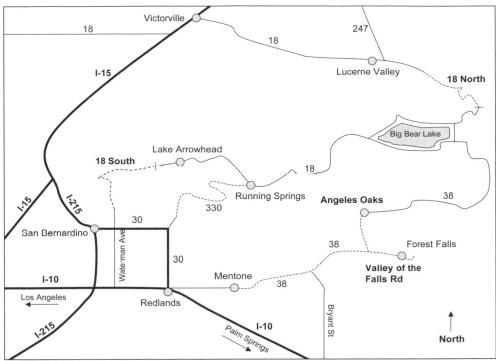

Valley of the Falls Rd, Angeles Oaks and 330, CA

Map labels:
- Victorville
- 18
- 18
- 247
- I-15
- Lucerne Valley
- **18 North**
- Big Bear Lake
- Lake Arrowhead
- **18 South**
- 18
- I-15
- I-215
- Running Springs
- Angeles Oaks
- 38
- 330
- San Bernardino
- 30
- Waterman Ave
- Forest Falls
- 30
- 38
- Mentone
- **Valley of the Falls Rd**
- I-10
- Los Angeles
- Redlands
- 38
- I-215
- I-10
- Palm Springs
- Bryant St
- North

Heading up toward Valley of the Falls and Angeles Oaks

eases. The listed climb ends at the junction with route 18 in the small town of Running Springs, CA. This is a fun but somewhat dangerous descent due to traffic and multiple hairpin turns.

Directions - From Interstate 10 in Redlands, CA take route 30 north. In approximately 4 miles route 330 splits off to the right and the climb begins just before the road goes from 4 to 2 lanes.

Facilities - San Bernardino, CA   **Airport** - Palm Springs, CA

18 (south)

Total elevation - 4,214 ft	**Length - 14.0 miles**
Average Grade - 5.7% (10%)	**Rating - 2.50 (cat 1)**

18 South carries a lot of traffic and is four lanes most of the way up with the first half of the route carrying the steepest grade. There are good views near the top and the climb ends in the small community of Crest Forest.

Directions - From I-10 in San Bernardino take route 18 (Waterman Ave) north for 4-5 miles to its intersection with 48th Street where the climb begins.

Facilities - San Bernardino, CA   **Airport** - Palm Springs, CA

18 (north)

Total elevation - 3,647 ft	**Length - 11.1 miles**
Average Grade - 6.2% (14%)	**Rating - 2.45 (cat 1)**

The north side of route 18 is a tough and isolated climb out of the desert up toward the Big Bear Lake area. Between fairly shallow top and bottom sections, the middle section is very tough and twisty with one extremely steep section. The climb ends at an unmarked pass just before you descend toward Baldwin Lake. This road carries a lot less traffic than the south side of route 18.

Directions - From Victorville, CA take route 18 east through the small town of Lucerne Valley. Continue east, past the junction of route 247, to Midway Ave (left). The climb begins just beyond Midway Ave as the grade increases up the hill.

Facilities - Victorville, CA   **Airport** - Palm Springs, CA

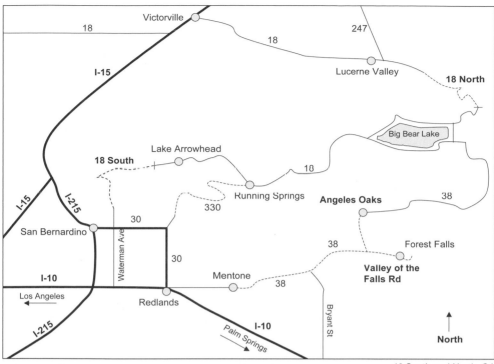

18 South and North, CA

Substituting is a big switchback on the climb to Onion Valley in the Sierras

N4/Table Mountain

Total elevation - 3,945 ft   Length - 13.9 miles

Average Grade - 5.4% (11%)   Rating - 2.33 (cat 1)

This climb starts out shallow and gradually gets steeper as it heads into a drainage. At the stop sign (mile 6.1) turn left toward Wrightwood. At the intersection with route 2 (Angeles Crest Highway) at mile 12.7 turn left and immediately take another left up to Table Mountain picnic area. This 1.2 mile finishing stretch is steeper than the previous section and ends at the top of a parking lot.

Directions - On route 18 in Victorville, CA head west through the high desert to the junction of 138 and 18. Continue west on 138 for another 1.5 miles to N4 (Largo Vista Rd) on the left where the climb begins.

Facilities - Victorville, CA   **Airport** - Palm Springs, CA

N4/Blue Ridge Summit

Total elevation - 3,963 ft   Length - 14.6 miles

Average Grade - 5.1% (9%)   Rating - 2.24 (cat 1)

This climb starts out shallow and gradually gets steeper as it enters a canyon. At the stop sign (mile 6.1) turn left toward the town of Wrightwood. At the intersection with route 2 (Angeles Crest Highway) at mile 12.7 turn right and climb for another 1.9 miles to the signed Blue Ridge Summit (7386 ft).

Directions - On route 18 in Victorville, CA head west through the high desert to the junction of 138 and 18. Continue west on 138 for 1.5 miles to N4 (Largo Vista Rd on the left) where the climb begins.

Facilities - Victorville, CA   **Airport** - Palm Springs, CA

138/Lone Pine Canyon/Table Mountain

Total elevation - 4,248 ft   Length - 15.8 miles

Average Grade - 5.1% (12%)   Rating - 2.38 (cat 1)

From just west of I-15 head up 138 along a shallow grade to begin the climb. At mile 1.0 turn left on Lone Pine Canyon Rd. Follow this very scenic section to the town of Wrightwood, making several turns once in town to end up at route 2 (Angeles Crest Highway). Turn left on route 2 and climb for 4 miles to the junction with N4 (on the right). At that junction turn right

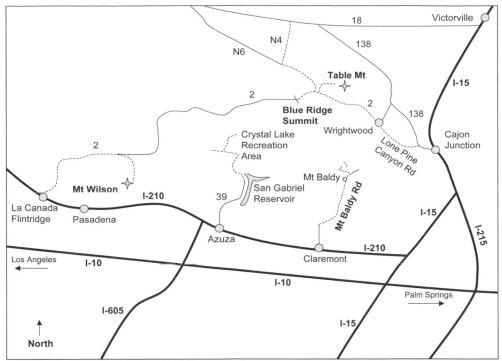

N4/Table Mtn, N4/Blue Ridge Summit and 138/ Lone Pine Canyon/Table Mtn, CA

Blue Ridge Summit near Los Angeles

(just before you reach N4) to climb up to Table Mtn where the climb ends at the top of a parking area.

Directions - From the junction of I-15 and I-215 near San Bernardino, CA head north on I-15 for ~8 miles to route 138 and head west. The climb begins at a dip just west of the interstate.

Facilities - San Bernardino, CA   **Airport** - Los Angeles, CA

138/Lone Pine Canyon/Blue Ridge Summit

Total elevation - 4,266 ft	Length - 17.7 miles
Average Grade - 4.6% (10%)	Rating - 2.30 (cat 1)

From just west of I-15 head up 138 along a shallow grade. At mile 1.0 turn left on Lone Pine Canyon Rd. Follow this very scenic section to the town of Wrightwood, making several turns once in town to end up at route 2 (Angeles Crest Highway). Turn left on route 2 and climb for four miles, passing the junction with N4 (on the right). Continue on route 2 up to the finish at Blue Ridge Summit (7,386 ft).

Directions - From the junction of I-15 and I-215 near San Bernardino, CA head north for ~8 miles to route 138 and head west. The climb begins on 138 at a dip just west of the interstate.

Facilities – San Bernardino, CA   **Airport** – Los Angeles, CA

Mount Baldy

Total elevation - 4,775 ft	Length - 12.9 miles
Average Grade - 7.0% (15%)	Rating - 3.57 (hors)

This is perhaps the toughest climb in Southern California along a scenic two lane road with a variable grade. The first few miles are fairly shallow with one steeper ramp. The grade increases just after the two short tunnels which appear around the five mile mark. You soon reach the village of Mount Baldy where the grade eases back a bit. Just beyond the village however the true nature of the hill reveals itself as the last 4 miles average almost 9% (turn left at mile 9.7 toward the ski area to finish). This final section contains ramps of 12-14% through steep switchbacks. The climb ends at the top section of a parking area. Mount Baldy is significantly longer and almost as steep as the famous Tourmalet in France.

Directions - From I-210 in Claremont, CA exit at Baseline Ave and head west a short distance to Mills Ave. Go right on Mills Ave for ~1.1 miles to its intersection with Mt Baldy Rd where the climb begins (parking area for cars).

Facilities - Claremont, CA   **Airport** - Los Angeles, CA

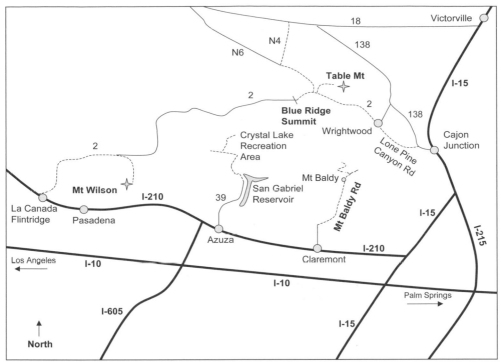

138/Lone Pine Canyon Rd/Blue Ridge Summit and Mt. Baldy, CA

A tough hairpin turn near the top of Mt. Baldy

Total elevation - 4,116 ft	Length - 15.8 miles
Average Grade - 4.9% (8%)	Rating - 2.12 (cat 1)

Route 39 is a nice climb into the San Gabriel Mountains with excellent views at its dead end.

Directions - From I-10 in West Covina, CA take route 39 (Azusa Ave) north. Ride through and beyond the town of Azusa and up into San Gabriel Canyon. The road climbs and then descends down to San Gabriel Reservoir. The climb begins at the end of the reservoir by continuing up the hill on 39.

Facilities - Azusa, CA	**Airport** - Los Angeles, CA

39/Crystal Lake

Total elevation - 4,295 ft	Length - 15.3 miles
Average Grade - 5.3% (9%)	Rating - 2.39 (cat 1)

This climb shares much of its length with route 39 (see previous climb). At mile 13 turn right up to Crystal Lake Recreation Area and climb as far as the pavement will allow (road ends at a parking area/campground).

Directions - From I-10 in West Covina, CA take route 39 (Azusa Ave) north. Ride through and beyond the town of Azusa and up into San Gabriel Canyon. The road climbs and then descends down to San Gabriel Reservoir. The climb begins at the end of the reservoir by continuing up the hill on 39.

Facilities - Azusa, CA	**Airport** - Los Angeles, CA

Mount Wilson

Total elevation - 4,330 ft	Length - 18.4 miles
Average Grade - 4.5% (10%)	Rating - 2.02 (cat 1)

Four lanes with a lot of traffic to start, Angeles Crest Rd soon turns to two lanes and becomes more scenic as it heads up into the San Gabriel Mountains. At mile 13.7 turn right on Mount Wilson Rd. The climb crests near roads end under the antennas with great views of the Los Angeles basin on clear days.

Directions - From I-210 in La Canada Flintridge exit on route 2 (Angeles Crest Rd). The climb begins at the intersection.

Facilities - Los Angeles, CA	**Airport** - Los Angeles, CA

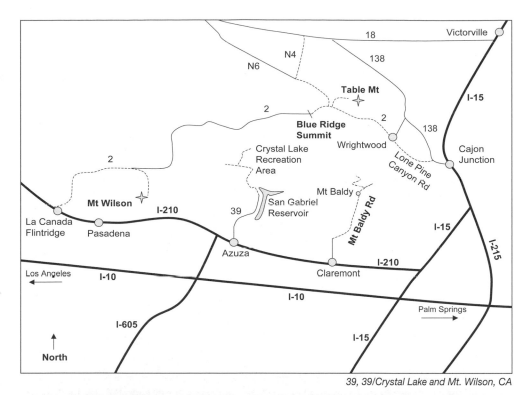

39, 39/Crystal Lake and Mt. Wilson, CA

Substituting is the top of Rose Summit near Lake Tahoe

Fargo Street

Length - 1/10 mile   **Average Grade - 32.5% (35%)**

Located in the Echo Park neighborhood of Los Angeles, Fargo Street is often referred to as the steepest street in the U.S. Although plenty steep it is not the steepest but very close (see list in appendices). It is used for unofficial races at times and will have you shaking at its end, whether you make it or not.

Directions - From the intersection of 101 and I-5 in Los Angeles, CA head south on I-5. At its junction with route 2 turn right or south. Soon the freeway ends and just beyond you turn left on Allesandro. After a very short drive the base of Fargo St appears on your right where the climb begins.

Facilities - Los Angeles, CA   **Airport** - Los Angeles, CA

Eldred Street

Length - 1/10 mile   **Average Grade - 32% (33%)**

The city of LA claims this is the steepest street in the city. Not as famous as Fargo St, Eldred will drill you as you head up to its dead end. The local dogs will help you to the top.

Directions - From the intersection of I-5 and I-110 in Los Angeles, CA head east on I-110 and exit at South Avenue 52. Head north on this road for a short distance and turn left on North Figueroa St. Travel west a short distance and then turn right on South Avenue 50. Eldred St will soon appear on your left. Head down Eldred a short distance and you cannot miss the climb.

Facilities - Los Angeles, CA   **Airport** - Los Angeles, CA

Baxter Street

Length - 1/10 mile   **Average Grade - 31% (32%)**

Another viciously steep hill, Baxter runs parallel to Fargo but this section is just south of Fargo's steep section.

Directions - From the intersection of 101 and I-5 in Los Angeles, CA head south on I-5. At its junction with route 2 turn right or south. Soon the freeway ends and just beyond you turn left on Allesandro. After a very short drive and just past Fargo St, Baxter will be on your right. Go up the hill (steep) to Alvarado. Head down the hill and turn around to climb the steepest section of Baxter.

Facilities - Los Angeles, CA   **Airport** - Los Angeles, CA

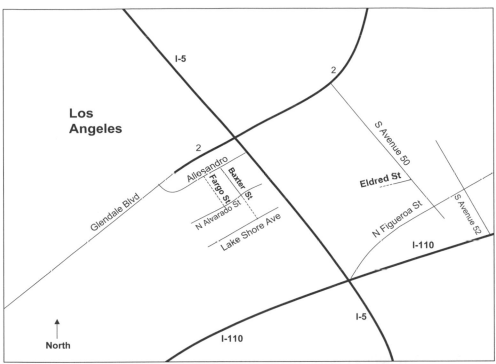

Fargo St, Eldred St and Baxter St, Los Angeles, CA

Looking up Fargo Street, one of steepest grades on earth

Mount Pinos

Total elevation - 4,400 ft

Length - 20.3 miles

Average Grade - 4.1% (10%)

Rating - 2.04 (cat 1)

From I-5 head up Frazier Mountain Rd through the town of Frazier Park. Just beyond town the grade eases and you bear right on Cuddy Valley Rd. This is a shallow stretch of climbing. After about five miles the grade increases again. The last section is classic mountain climbing through big trees along a twisty route. The climb dead ends at a parking area near the top of Mount Pinos (8,300 ft).

Directions - Head to Frazier Park, CA just north of Los Angeles on I-5. The climb begins at the junction of I-5 and Frazier Mountain Rd. Head west on Frazier Mountain Rd to begin the climb.

Facilities - Bakersfield, CA

Airport - Bakersfield, CA

San Marcos/Painted Cave Road

Total elevation - 2,485 ft

Length - 5.5 miles

Average Grade - 8.6% (20%)

Rating - 2.20 (cat 1)

This is a very difficult and scenic climb up into the coast mountains above Santa Barbara, CA. After three miles on San Marcos go straight at the stop sign (intersection with route 154) to Painted Cave Rd. This road has big switchbacks with double digit grade, dark, single lane sections and a short stretch of 20% near the top where the road dead-ends. This is a classic west coast climb.

Directions - From route 101 between Santa Barbara and Goleta, CA head east on Turnpike Rd. At Cathedral Oaks turn left for a short distance and then turn right on San Marcos. Head up San Marcos to the bridge over the creek just beyond Via Parva Rd (right) where the climb begins.

Facilities - Santa Barbara, CA

Airport - Santa Barbara, CA

Gilbraltor Road

Total elevation - 3,560 ft

Length - 10.2 miles

Average Grade - 6.6% (11%)

Rating - 2.40 (cat 1)

Gibraltor Rd is a difficult and scenic climb with great views of the Channel Islands out in the Pacific Ocean. In Santa Barbara, take Mountain Dr up the hill and stay on Mountain Dr by

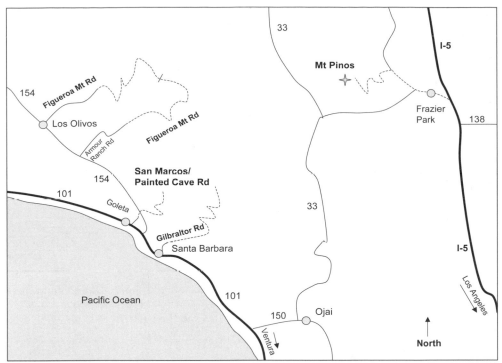

Mt. Pinos, San Marcos/Painted Cave Rd and Gilbraltor Rd, CA

A double digit grade hairpin turn on Painted Cave Rd

turning left at the reservoir. After another 2/10's of a mile turn right on Gilbraltor Rd which takes you all the way to the top along a very twisty route. The top is along poor pavement and the climb ends (unmarked) by the building with antennas on your left.

Directions - From Highway 101 in Santa Barbara, CA exit onto Mission St. Follow Mission St east to Mission Canyon Rd. Continue east on Mission Canyon Rd and a short distance later Mountain Dr takes off from the right which is where the climb begins.

Facilities - Santa Barbara, CA   **Airport** - Santa Barbara, CA

Figueroa Mountain Road (east)

Total elevation - 3,342 ft	**Length** - 9.7 miles
Average Grade - 6.5% (11%)	**Rating** - 2.29 (cat 1)

The east side of Figueroa Mountain Rd is a very solid climb into the coastal mountains. A less variable climb than the west side, there is a dirt section of this hill near the bottom that lasts for 9/10ths mile. Great views arrive near the top and the climb ends at an unmarked summit.

Directions - From route 154 in Los Olivos, CA, head east through town to Armour Ranch Rd on the left. Head up this road for 1.2 miles and turn right on Happy Canyon Rd. The hill begins 7.3 miles up this road (and becomes Figueroa Mt Rd).

Facilities - Santa Barbara, CA   **Airport** - Santa Barbara, CA

Figueroa Mountain Road (west)

Total elevation - 3,146 ft	**Length** - 9.6 miles
Average Grade - 6.2% (15%)	**Rating** - 2.00 (cat 1)

The west side Figueroa Mountain Rd is a classic ride. It is very scenic, with very steep ramps and a few descents. It resembles some European mountain roads as it is a wide single lane in spots, has several steep hairpin turns and is poorly paved for part of its length. It is also extensively used by professional cycling teams for off season training including Lance Armstrong's Discovery Channel team.

Directions - From route 154 in Los Olivos, CA, Figueroa Mountain Rd heads north and is well marked. Follow the road for 6.8 miles to a 90 degree right turn and a single lane bridge over a creek where the listed climb begins.

Facilities - Santa Barbara, CA   **Airport** - Santa Barbara, CA

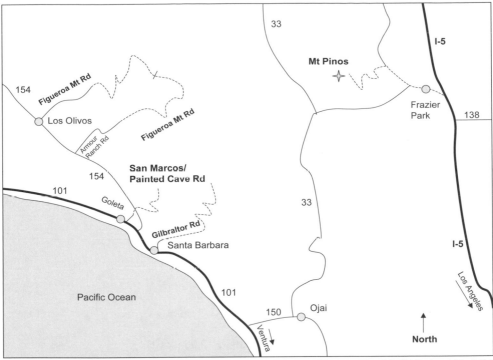

Figueroa Mountain Rd East and West, CA

A steep hairpin on the west side of Figueroa Mountain Rd

Nacimiento Fergusson Road (west)

Total elevation - 2,506 ft	Length - 6.9 miles
Average Grade - 6.9% (11%)	Rating - 1.74 (cat 1)

The west side of Nacimiento Fergusson Rd is included as it is a solid climb that is perhaps the most scenic in the U.S. on an isolated road with great views of the Pacific Ocean. Very narrow without any shoulder over much of its length, the top section is shaded. The east side of this climb is single lane in places and winds through a tunnel of trees.

Directions - From San Luis Obispo, CA head north on highway 1. Nacimiento Fergusson Rd is on your right about halfway between San Simeon and Big Sur.

Facilities - Monterey, CA   Airport - Monterey, CA

Bohlman Road/On Orbit Drive

Total elevation - 1,557 ft	Length - 2.3 miles
Average Grade - 12.8% (21%)	Rating - 2.05 (cat 1)

From the cemetery this road heads up hill at a modest incline but soon becomes very steep. About halfway up, there is a section of 21% grade within a series of switchbacks through one of the most difficult miles of climbing in the U.S. At the 'T' go left on On Orbit and another ramp of 20%. At mile 2.2 turn left on Apollo where the climb soon dead ends.

Directions - From the intersection of route 9 and 6th Street in Saratoga, CA head south on 6th to Bohlman Rd (cemetery ahead and to the right). At the intersection go right on Bohlman Rd and the climb begins in 2/10ths mile.

Facilities - Saratoga, CA   Airport - San Jose, CA

Bohlman Road

Total elevation - 1,648 ft	Length - 2.6 miles
Average Grade - 12.0% (21%)	Rating - 2.04 (cat 1)

Identical to the above climb but at the 'T' go right to stay on Bohlman Rd. The climb ends at an old county park. The road continues but rolls up and down and eventually the pavement ends.

Directions - See previous climb.

Facilities - Saratoga, CA   Airport - San Jose, CA

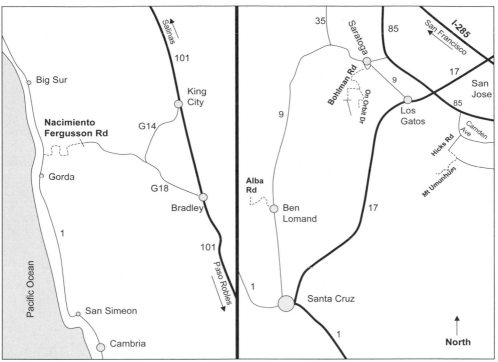

Nacimiento Fergusson Rd, Bohlman/On Orbit and Bohlman Rd, CA

The Pacific Coast seen from Nacimiento Fergusson Rd

Alba Road

Total elevation - 2,030 ft	Length - 3.8 miles
Average Grade - 10.2% (19%)	Rating - 2.14 (cat 1)

Alba Rd is a very steep, short and scenic climb through stands of big redwoods. A variable grade will grind you down.

Directions - From Santa Cruz, CA take route 9 north to the small town of Ben Lomand. Alba Rd takes off to the left in the middle of town.

Facilities - Santa Cruz, CA   **Airport** - San Jose, CA

Hicks Road/Mount Umunhum

Total elevation - 2,160 ft	Length - 4.1 miles
Average Grade - 10.0% (18%)	Rating - 2.18 (cat 1)

This hill is very steep and scenic. After Hicks Rd crests (in one mile), descend a very short distance and turn right on Mt. Umunhum. Continue through another very steep mile and soon a gate appears. Climb over the gate and ride 1.2 miles to the end of the legal road.

Directions - From the corner of Camden Ave and Hicks Rd in San Jose, CA head west on Hicks for ~5 miles of shallow climbing. The listed climb begins where the grade increases.

Facilities - San Jose, CA   **Airport** - San Jose, CA

Marin Avenue

Length/Average Grade (half mile) - 18.1% (28%); (mile) - 14.1% (28%)

Marin Avenue may contain the most difficult half and full mile of climbing in the U.S. It is not the steepest in either category but throw in stop signs, traffic and leg numbing grade variability and you will see why it is more difficult than its statistics suggest. For the full mile, enjoy the first 1/10 mile as it is the only break you will get. Negotiate 'The Circle' and your real troubles begin as you slam into sustained 20% grade. The only forgiveness comes from the cross street sections which are flat. At Santa Barbara (cross street) the real fun begins as you hit the steepest half mile of the climb. After 8/10ths mile the grade finally eases and you finish the torture fittingly at a seminary at the top of the hill. Good luck with this one!

Directions - From I-80 in Berkeley, CA, take the Buchanan Street exit toward Albany. Head east on Buchanan for a half mile which becomes Marin Avenue. Follow Marin for 1.5 miles to begin the climb by continuing east.

Facilities - Berkeley, CA   **Airport** - Oakland, CA

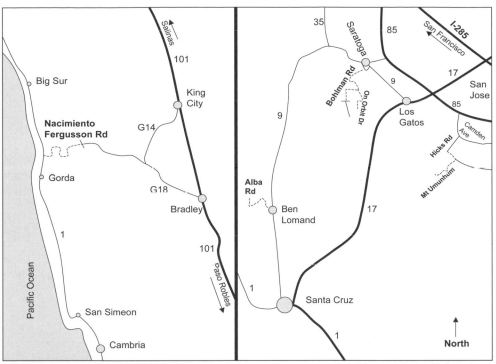

Alba Rd and Hicks/Mt. Umunhum, CA

Near the top of the very steep first mile of Hicks/Mt Umunhum

Colorado

Trail Ridge (east)

Total elevation - 4,661 ft

Length - 18.2 miles

Average Grade - 4.8% (8%)

Rating - 2.83 (hors/cat 1)

Trail Ridge is a very spectacular climb into Rocky Mountain National Park. After several miles you pass through the entrance gate ($5 for bikes as of 2005). Near the top the setting is tundra-like with great mountain views as you top out at Trail Ridge (12,183 ft). Don't underestimate the elevation attained on this climb. Due to its elevation it has a pretty short window to ride and does carry a lot of traffic so ride early in the day if possible (closed in winter – Rocky Mountain National Park 970 586-1206). The west side climb is 26.5 miles at a grade of 2.7% beginning at Grand Lake Village, CO.

Directions - The climb begins at the western edge of Estes Park, CO at the last traffic light before leaving town on route 36. Head up route 36 (which will turn into Route 34) to begin.

Facilities - Estes Park, CO

Airport - Denver, CO

Mount Evans

Total elevation - 6,590 ft

Length - 27.8 miles

Average Grade - 4.5% (10%)

Rating - 3.88 (hors)

The road on Mount Evans is the highest paved road in the northwestern hemisphere and the most difficult and spectacular climb in Colorado. Never very steep, the altitude will work on you all the way up. After 13.2 miles and just past Echo Lake you turn right to pass through an entrance station ($3 per bike as of 2007) for the push to the summit. The road gets very narrow at this point as you head above the treeline. There are several small descents before you reach Summit Lake Park at mile 21.5. From here the road heads up through switchbacks with amazing views. At the top (14,130 ft) you will find an overlook and restrooms. You must hike the final bit to reach the very top of the mountain. Be careful on the descent as there are no guardrails in places and it is often very windy. Due to its altitude this road has a short window for use, usually opening by early June and closing sometime in September. It also carries a lot of traffic on good weather days so you will likely have company on your ascent so start early in the day. The toll booth is not manned after the road is closed in the Fall. This is a must do ride for serious hill climbers (closed in winter – Arapaho National Forest 303 567-3000).

Directions - From I-70 in Idaho Springs, CO take exit 240 for route 103. Head south on 103 and you immediately come to the Clear Creek Ranger Station on the right. The climb begins here.

Facilities - Denver, CO

Airport - Denver, CO

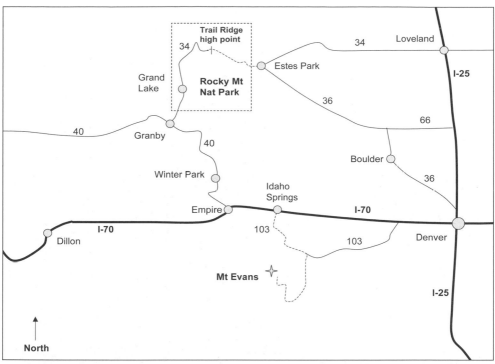

Trail Ridge East and Mt. Evans, CO

A lone rider struggles above 13,000 ft on Mt. Evans

The super steep Hurricane Mountain Rd in New Hampshire

Above treeline on massive Mt. Evans in Colorado

The very scenic Nacimiento Fergusson Rd in California

The stacked switchbacks of spectacular Onion Valley Rd

The very scenic Salt River Canyon in Arizona

A warning of things to come in the Sierras

A big switchback on North Carolina's Beech Mountain

Climbing out of Zion National Park in Utah

Near the beginning of massive Horseshoe Meadows in California

The spectacular east side of Independence Pass in Colorado

Heading up to Lake Sabrina in the eastern Sierras

The scenery along the climb to Antelope Pass in Arizona

Approaching 20% grade on Vermont's Burke Mountain

Climbing out of the Kings River gorge in California

The Rocky Mountains as you climb to Loveland Pass

Approaching the mighty Sierras

The twisty route up to Colorado National Monument

Getting high

Single lane above 10,000 feet in the Sierras

Juniper Pass (west)

Total Elevation - 3,590 ft　　　　　Length - 15.9 miles

Average Grade - 4.3% (9%)　　　　Rating - 1.87 (cat 1)

This climb shares its beginning with Mount Evans (previous climb). At mile 13.2 (junction to Mount Evans) continue straight on 103. The hill crests 2.7 miles later at an unmarked pass (11,130 ft). This high point on the road is not the actual Juniper Pass which is a ridge crest one mile behind you (and several hundred feet lower). The east side of Juniper Pass is 16.1 miles at 4% beginning near Bergen Park, CO.

Directions - On I-70 in Idaho Springs, CO take exit 240 for route 103. Just after exiting you come to the Clear Creek Ranger Station on the right. The climb begins here.

Facilities - Denver, CO　　　　　**Airport** - Denver, CO

Loveland Pass (south)

Total elevation - 2,533 ft　　　　　Length - 8.3 miles

Average Grade - 5.8% (10%)　　　　Rating - 1.83 (cat 1)

The south side of Loveland Pass is a solid climb up past a ski resort to very good views from the pass (11,992 ft). The north side is a very scenic climb (4.2 miles at 5.4%).

Directions - From Keystone, CO take route 6 east to Montezuma Rd (on the right) where the climb begins.

Facilities - Dillon, CO　　　　　**Airport** - Denver, CO

Independence Pass (west)

Total elevation - 3,991 ft　　　　　Length - 15.9 miles

Average Grade - 4.7% (8%)　　　　Rating - 2.37 (cat 1)

The first several miles of this climb are along a two lane road through thick trees. Higher up the road turns to a single lane and hugs a cliff with great views. Returning to two lanes, a very scenic alpine section takes you up to the pass at 12,095 ft (closed in winter - San Isabel National Forest - 719 539-3591). The east side is a very scenic climb from Twin Lakes, CO (17.4 miles at 3.1%).

Directions - From Aspen, CO head east on route 82. After ~3.5 miles you will see a sign and parking area for the White River National Forest on the right. The climb begins here.

Facilities - Aspen, CO　　　　　**Airport** - Aspen, CO

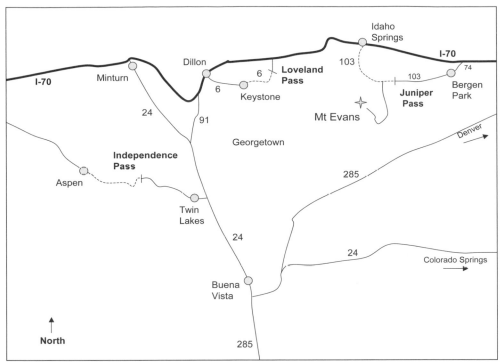

Juniper Pass West, Loveland Pass South and Independence Pass West, CO

Heading up to scenic Independence Pass

Pikes Peak

Total elevation - 3,872 ft	Length - 15.7 miles
Average Grade - 4.7% (10%)	Rating - 2.06 (cat 1)

Unfortunately this climb is closed to bikes. After 5.3 miles on route 24 turn left on Pikes Peak Highway. Soon after, keep left at a fork in the road. The grade soon increases and you pass the tollbooth for cars. A very steep mile follows and then the road levels off through meadows and trees. Passing a lake on the left, great views of the mountain appear. After another few miles the road turns to gravel. Once this entire climb is paved (planned) it will become one of the top 5 most difficult in the U.S.

Directions - From I-25 in Colorado Springs, CO head west on route 24. After several miles you will come to the town of Manitou and the intersection with Manitou Rd. The climb begins here by continuing west on 4-lane route 24.

Facilities - Colorado Springs, CO   **Airport** - Denver, CO

Cottonwood Pass

Total elevation - 4,173 ft	Length - 18.7 miles
Average Grade - 4.2% (10%)	Rating - 2.20 (cat 1)

A solid climb up to an alpine pass (12,126 ft). The road turns to dirt at the top (closed in winter - San Isabel National Forest - 719 539-3591).

Directions - From Route 24 in Buena Vista, CO head west on Route 306. The climb begins at the western city limits at the junction with Route 321 on the left.

Facilities – Buena Vista, CO   **Airport** – Aspen, CO

Monarch Pass (west)

Total elevation - 2,849 ft	Length - 9.9 miles
Average Grade - 5.5% (7%)	Rating - 1.90 (cat 1)

Shorter and steeper than the approach from the east, this road carries some traffic. The east side of Monarch is a solid climb of 17.6 miles at 4.1% grade.

Directions - From Gunnison, CO head east on route 50 to the small town of Sargents where the climb begins.

Facilities - Salida, CO   **Airport** - Colorado Springs, CO

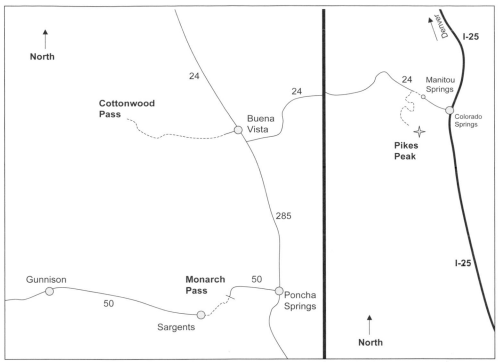

Pikes Peak, Cottonwood Pass and Monarch Pass West, CO

Colorado's massive Pikes Peak

Slumgullion Pass (west)

Total elevation - 2,476 ft	Length - 7.7 miles
Average Grade - 6.1% (9%)	Rating - 1.86 (cat 1)

The west side of Slumgullion Pass is an isolated, high altitude climb (11,530 ft) with a grade that will make you work. The east side is short and shallow (5.2 miles at 3.8%).

Directions - From Lake City, CO head south on route 149 to the bridge over the Lake Fork of the Gunnison River where the climb begins.

Facilities - Gunnison, CO   **Airport** - Grand Junction, CO

Red Mountain Pass (north)

Total elevation - 3,311 ft	Length - 13.4 miles
Average Grade - 4.7% (9%)	Rating - 1.89 (cat 1)

This side of Red Mountain is a very spectacular climb up a twisty road to a high altitude pass (11,081 ft). This road carries a fair amount of traffic at times but may be the most scenic, high mountain road in the U.S. The south side of Red Mountain Pass is also very scenic (9.8 miles at 3.4% from Silverton, CO).

Directions - From the hot springs in downtown Ouray, CO head south on 550 to begin the climb.

Facilities - Montrose, CO   **Airport** - Grand Junction, CO

East Portal

Total elevation - 1,915 ft	Length - 3.1 miles
Average Grade - 11.7% (16%)	Rating - 2.60 (cat 1)

East Portal is a very steep and scenic climb up from the Gunnison River within Black Canyon of the Gunnison National Park. From the river head uphill. The first two miles are very steep and contain the maximum grade on this climb. The listed climb ends after 3.1 miles at an unmarked top (the road continues to climb intermittently but along very shallow grade).

Directions - From Montrose, CO head east on route 50 for eight miles to route 347 on the left. Take 347 up into the park. At the entrance station turn right on East Portal. Head down all the way to the river and take a left on the road to the ranger residences. After 1/10 mile, turn around to begin the climb by heading out of the canyon.

Facilities - Montrose, CO   **Airport** - Grand Junction, CO

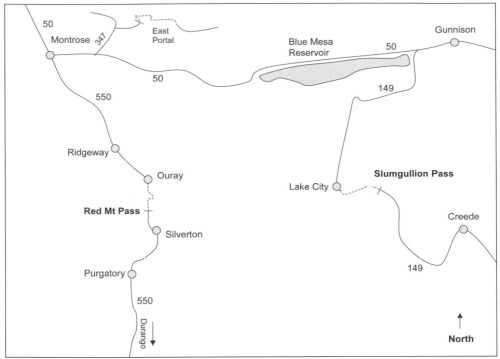

Slumgullion Pass West, Red Mountain Pass North and East Portal, CO

The very steep route up East Portal

Grand Mesa (north)

Total elevation - 5,622 ft	Length - 21.4 miles
Average Grade - 5.0% (8%)	Rating - 3.39 (hors/cat 1)

This may be the second most difficult climb in CO. Soon after starting you head through the town of Mesa along route 65 on a straight stretch of road. Eventually you start to switchback up to the high country. The climb that ends on top of Grand Mesa (10,852 ft) at the border of Mesa and Delta counties.

Directions - From Grand Junction, CO head east on I-70 to route 65 (exit 49). Head south on 65 for ten miles to its junction with route 330 (on the left) to begin the climb.

Facilities - Grand Junction, CO **Airport** - Grand Junction, CO

Grand Mesa (south)

Total elevation - 4,752 ft	Length - 20.7 miles
Average Grade - 4.4% (7%)	Rating - 2.50 (cat 1)

This side of Grand Mesa is a very long and scenic climb. Unspectacular lower end gives way to ridge views and lakes once into the National Forest. You pass Grand Mesa Lodge near the top and the climb ends at the Mesa County line.

Directions - From Delta, CO head east on route 92 to route 65. Turn left on 65, cross the Gunnison River bridge and travel ~9 miles to the small town of Cedaredge where the climb begins at the intersection with Main Street.

Facilities - Delta, CO **Airport** - Grand Junction, CO

Colorado National Monument (east)

Total elevation - 1,900 ft	Length - 8.4 miles
Average Grade - 4.3% (8%)	Rating - 0.88 (cat 2)

Made famous in the movie American Flyers, this climb up the east side of the Monument is very scenic, passing through a short tunnel. There is a gate near the bottom which if manned will charge you $3 for the climb (2007). At mile 7.1 turn left toward Glade Park Store to continue to climb. The hill ends 1.3 miles later at an unmarked crest.

Directions - In Grand Junction, CO head to the corner of Monument Dr and route 340 to begin the climb.

Facilities - Grand Junction, CO **Airport** - Grand Junction, CO

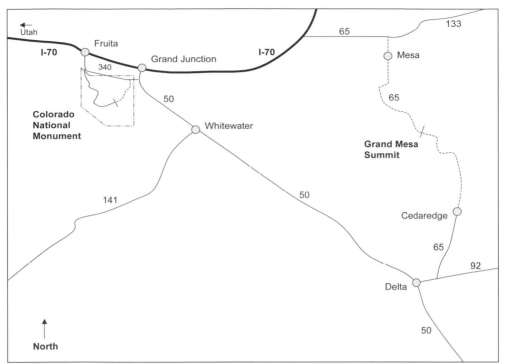

Grand Mesa North and South and Colorado National Monument East, CO

A scenic switchback along the climb up the east side of Colorado National Monument

Hawaii

Haleakala

Total elevation - 9,997 ft	Length - 36.5 miles
Average Grade - 5.2% (10%)	Rating - 6.13 (hors)

Haleakala is a classic road bike climb and among the most difficult in the world. From the corner of Hana Highway and Baldwin Ave in the small town of Paia on the island of Maui, head up an easy grade for 7.1 miles to the town of Makewao. At the intersection with Makewao Ave go straight up the hill as Baldwin Ave becomes Olinda (do not turn right on Makewao Ave as some suggest. This adds 1.5 miles of flat riding within much more traffic). Climb for one mile on Olinda and turn right on Hanamu for another mile to the junction of route 377. Turn left on 377 for five miles to its junction with 378. Turn left on 378 which will take you the rest of the way up (only 7,000 ft to go!). The road soon begins to switchback up the mountain, crossing four cattle guards along the way. Just beyond the forth one you come to the National Park entrance gate where you must stop and pay $5 (yes, even bikes). The Visitors Center is one mile further up the road (water). The terrain becomes rocky at this point with great views on a clear day. Continue climbing up to the upper visitor's center where you turn right. The climb finishes at the shelter at 10,023 ft (ride up the paved trail to the very top). This climb is so long make sure you take plenty of food and fluids. The descent is wild but can be cold (and wet) so carry what you might need.

Directions - On the island of Maui head to the small town of Paia and the corner of Hana Highway and Baldwin Ave. The climb begins by heading up Baldwin Ave.

Facilities - Kahului, HI	**Airport** - Kahului, HI

Baldwin Avenue/Olinda Road

Total elevation - 4,034 ft	Length - 12.7 miles
Average Grade - 6.0% (11%)	Rating - 2.48 (cat 1)

This climb shares its beginning with Haleakala. One mile beyond the town of Makewao, continue straight on Olinda instead of turning right on Hanamu. The road continues to climb with some steeper sections and dead ends.

Directions - On the island of Maui head to the small town of Paia and the corner of Hana Highway and Baldwin Ave. The climb begins by heading up Baldwin Ave.

Facilities - Kahului, HI	**Airport** - Kahului, HI

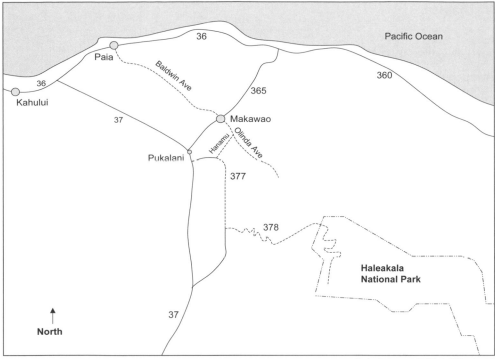

Haleakala and Baldwin/Olinda, HI

Heading through lava near the top of massive Haleakala

Mauna Kea

Total elevation - 9,117 ft	Length - 34.6 miles
Average Grade - 5.0% (16%)	Rating - 5.26 (hors)

Mauna Kea is one of the most difficult climbs in the world. After 1.25 miles in town turn left on Kaumana Rd (Saddle Rd). Rolling miles follow and lava eventually replaces trees as you ride between two massive volcanoes. Soon the grade eases and at mile 28 turn right for the top. This section is shallow and then gets steep including one of the hardest paved miles in the U.S. Just beyond you reach the Visitors Center (right) and the pavement and climb ends soon after. If and when the section to the top is paved it will become the world's toughest climb. It is tough enough as is so go prepared (there are no services once you leave Hilo).

Directions - In downtown Hilo, HI begin the climb at the corner of Waianuenue and route 19. The climb begins by heading up the hill on Waianuenue.

Facilities - Hilo, HI	**Airport** - Hilo, HI

Mauna Loa

Total elevation - 11,091 ft	Length - 44.8 miles
Average Grade - 4.7% (9%)	Rating - 6.33 (hors)

Mauna Loa is one of the most difficult climbs in the world that shares much of its length with Mauna Kea. Follow the Mauna Kea directions and at mile 27.7 turn left on a one lane, red colored road (unmarked as of 2/02. If you reach the Mauna Kea turnoff on the right you have gone too far). Shallow to start, the grade on this section gradually increases and the climb ends at a weather station (11,115 ft). This last stretch is isolated and not maintained. This may be the greatest continuous elevation-gain paved road hill climb on earth so go prepared.

Directions - See Mauna Kea above

Facilities - Hilo, HI	**Airport** - Hilo, HI

Stainback Road

Total elevation - 4,965 ft	Length - 18.7 miles
Average Grade - 5.2% (9%)	Rating - 2.58 (cat 1)

Stainback Road is a good warm-up for the giant climbs on the island.

Directions - From Hilo, HI go south on route 11 for ~ 4 miles to Stainback Rd (right).

Facilities - Hilo, HI	**Airport** - Hilo, HI

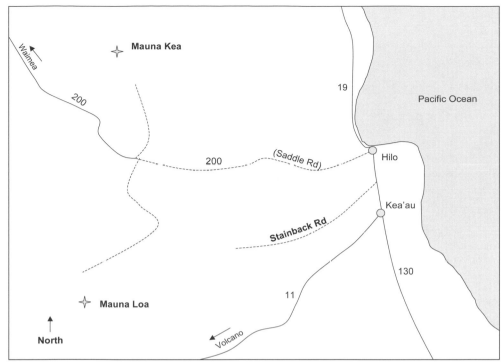

Mauna Kea, Mauna Loa and Stainback Rd, HI

The single lane road along the last section of giant Mauna Loa

Nevada

Rose Summit (north)

Total elevation - 4,349 ft	Length - 16.1 miles
Average Grade - 5.1% (10%)	Rating - 2.55 (cat 1)

From highway 395 this climb begins as a four lane road heading west. After about four miles it reduces to two lanes and soon starts to twist up the mountain toward Lake Tahoe. Fairly steady grade and with some good views near the top, it ends at Rose Summit (8,933 ft). The south side of this hill begins very near Lake Tahoe and is shorter and scenic (8.1 miles at 5.9%).

Directions - From Reno, NV head south on route 395 to its junction with South Virginia St. Head south on this road for a short distance to route 431 to begin the climb by heading west on 431.

Facilities - Reno, NV	Airport - Reno, NV

Wheeler Peak

Total elevation - 4,845 ft	Length - 15.6 miles
Average Grade - 5.9% (10%)	Rating - 3.39 (hors/cat 1)

Wheeler Peak is one of the most difficult climbs in Nevada and it's most spectacular. A very straight and steady-grade start greets you up this isolated hill with great views of usually snow-capped Wheeler Peak in Great Basin National Park. At mile 4.8 turn right on Wheeler Peak Scenic Drive (continue straight to get to the National Park Visitors Center). From this point the road is narrow and twisty and resembles an alpine climb. Great views soon appear as you head higher into stands of trees. The climb ends at Summit Trailhead (10,163 ft) with the massive mountain right in front of you. The paved road continues but descends down to a campground. This is a classic climb that few are aware of and is significantly longer and as steep as one route up the Col d'Izoard, a beyond category climb often used in the TdF (closed in winter - Great Basin National Park - 775 234-7331).

Directions - From route 487 in the small town of Baker, NV just east of Great Basin National Park head to the junction with route 488 where the climb begins by heading up 488 towards Great Basin National Park.

Facilities - Ely, NV	Airport - Salt Lake City, UT

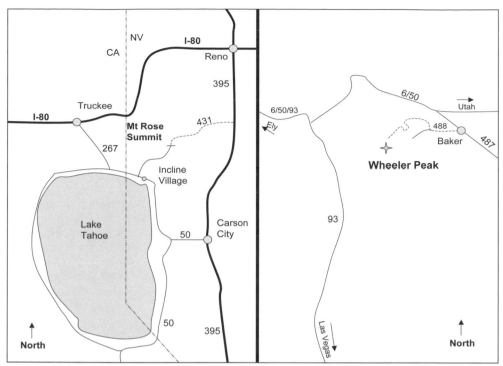

Rose Summit North and Wheeler Peak, NV

The top of mighty Wheeler Peak

Mount Charleston

Total elevation - 5,020 ft	Length - 21.2 miles
Average Grade - 4.5% (10%)	Rating - 2.50 (cat 1)

Mount Charleston (route 157) is a long and scenic climb into the Spring Mountains north of Las Vegas. From the junction of routes 95 and 157, head west up 157. The grade gradually increases and then flattens as you approach the junction with 158. Continue straight on 157. At mile 20.2 in the small community of Mount Charleston, turn right on Echo and begin a series of turns on one lane residential streets along much steeper grades. After 8/10ths mile on Echo turn right on Crestview. After 1/10th mile take a left on Kris Kringle and then a right on Snow White to finish at an unmarked summit. A great Fall/Winter/Spring ride (the occasional winter snow is quickly plowed), the bottom half is very hot in summer. Mount Charleston and the following three climbs will keep any peak bagger busy when visiting the Las Vegas area.

Directions - From Las Vegas, NV head north on route 95 for approximately 10 miles (as Las Vegas grows this distance is shrinking each year) to its junction with route 157 (on the left) where the climb begins.

Facilities - Las Vegas, NV	**Airport** - Las Vegas, NV

157/158

Total elevation - 5,621 ft	Length - 22.3 miles
Average Grade - 4.8% (10%)	Rating - 3.04 (hors/cat 1)

157/158 shares its start, and most of its length, with the Mt. Charleston climb (previous). After about eighteen miles on route 157 and along more shallow grade, turn right on Nevada 158. The climb immediately gets steeper at this point as it contours up and around the flank of the mountains with very good views down into the valley. It ends at a pullout with an elevation marker (8,437 ft). 158 carries very little traffic and is a very pleasant ride in itself as well. You can continue on route 158 to reach route 156 (next climb).

Directions - From Las Vegas, NV head north on route 95 for approximately 10 miles (as Las Vegas grows this distance is shrinking each year) to its junction with route 157 (on the left) where the climb begins.

Facilities - Las Vegas, NV	**Airport** - Las Vegas, NV

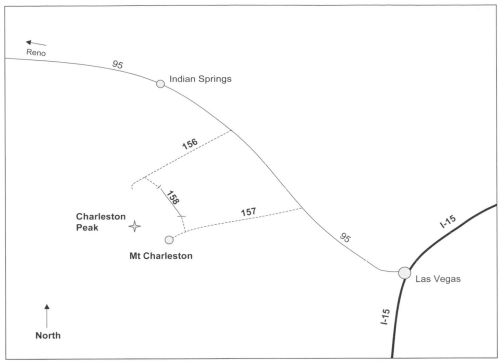

Mt. Charleston and 157/158, NV

Battling the elements and altitude on route 157/158, NV

Total elevation - 5,348 ft	Length - 17.3 miles
Average Grade - 5.9% (10%)	Rating - 3.57 (hors)

One of the toughest hill climbs in the U.S. and the most difficult in Nevada, 156 heads out of a desert valley on a very straight road which lets you see the agony to come. A very steady grade for most of its length, the bottom half is very hot in summer. Above 7000 feet, trees appear for a bit of shade in places and the grade eases slightly. Continue straight on 156 at the junction with 158 on the left. The climb ends at the top of a parking area for a ski resort (8,668 ft). Hang on for the descent as it may be the fastest in the U.S. There is an annual climbing race on its slopes as well.

Directions - From Las Vegas, NV head north on route 95 for approximately 25 miles (as Las Vegas grows this distance is shrinking each year) to route 156 (on the left) where the climb begins.

Facilities - Las Vegas, NV   **Airport** - Las Vegas, NV

156/158

Total elevation - 5,002 ft	Length - 16.1 miles
Average Grade - 5.9% (10%)	Rating - 3.32 (hors/cat 1)

Another very difficult climb, this hill shares route 156 (previous climb) until mile 13.9 when you turn left onto Nevada 158. Continue just over two miles from that junction to top out at an unmarked pass at 8,322 ft. After a descent the road continues to climb intermittently but significant climbing has ended. You can continue on lightly traveled route 158 to reach route 157 (Mount Charleston climb).

Directions - From Las Vegas, NV head north on route 95 for approximately 25 miles (as Las Vegas grows this distance is shrinking each year)to route 156 (on the left) where the climb begins.

Facilities - Las Vegas, NV   **Airport** - Las Vegas, NV

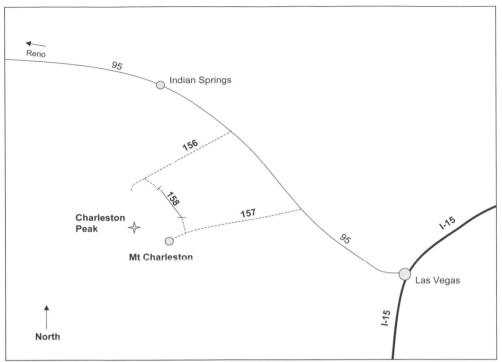

156 and 156/158, NV

Near the beginning of the tough climb up route 156 in Nevada

New Mexico

Sandia Crest

Total Elevation - 3,803 ft	Length - 13.5 miles
Average Grade - 5.3% (10%)	Rating - 2.44 (cat 1)

Sandia Crest is a solid climb up to high altitude and great views. After a shallow start, the road soon enters a spruce forest as it twists up the hill. There is a small descent near a ski area and then climbing continues, generally getting steeper as you go. The climb ends at a small parking area (10,661 ft). Hike a short distance to an overlook at the very top that is worth the effort. You can ride this hill all the way from Albuquerque but much of the route is very shallow climbing.

Directions - Head east on I-40 from Albuquerque, NM. Within a few miles take exit 175 for the town of Tijeras. At the bottom of the exit is a stoplight where you turn left on Route 133. After a half mile on 133 turn right (north) on route 14. After ~six miles route 536 appears. Turn left to begin the climb at the intersection of routes 14 and 536.

Facilities - Albuquerque, NM   **Airport** - Albuquerque, NM

Cloudcroft (west)

Total elevation - 3,957 ft	Length - 14.3 miles
Average Grade - 5.2% (9%)	Rating - 2.37 (cat 1)

The west side of Cloudcroft is a solid route up to the high country of southern New Mexico, ending in the small town of Cloudcroft. The statistics on this climb are estimates. The east side of this hill is a long and shallow ascent.

Directions - From Alamogordo, NM head north on route 54 for several miles to route 82 on your right. Head east on 82 for several miles to Florida Street on the right where the climb begins by continuing east on 82.

Facilities - Alamogordo, NM   **Airport** - El Paso, TX

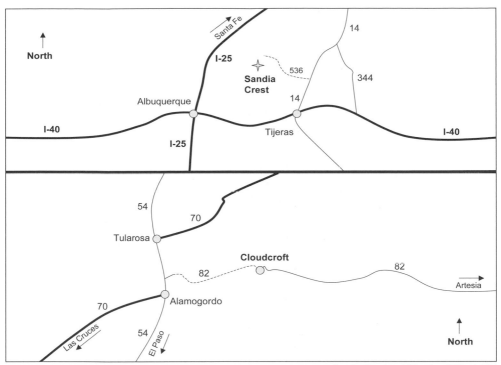

Sandia Crest and Cloudcroft West, NM

Substituting is the scenic route 120 near Yosemite National Park in California

Oregon

Mount Hood

Total elevation - 4,454 ft	Length - 15.0 miles
Average Grade - 5.6% (10%)	Rating - 2.65 (cat 1)

Begin by heading east on route 26 on a moderate grade with some traffic. At mile 9.7 (just past Government Camp) turn left toward Timberline Lodge. This final stretch is steeper and scenic. The climb ends at the top of the parking area with great views of massive Mt. Hood.

Directions - From Portland OR head east on route 26 to the tiny community of Rhododendron, OR, where the climb begins by continuing east on 26.

Facilities - Portland, OR   Airport - Portland, OR

Bear Camp Summit (west)

Total elevation - 4,280 ft	Length - 14.2 miles
Average Grade - 5.7% (11%)	Rating - 2.50 (cat 1)

One of the most isolated climbs in this guide, the west side of Bear Camp Summit is very scenic and single lane in places. The above stats are estimated (closed in winter - Siskiyou National Forest - 541 247-3600). The east side is an easier climb of ~3,700 ft over ~18 miles.

Directions - From Gold Beach, OR head east on route 33 for about twenty-eight miles to its intersection with route 23 (on the right). The climb begins by heading east on route 23.

Facilities - Medford, OR   Airport - Medford, OR

Mount Ashland

Total elevation - 4,308 ft	Length - 16.8 miles
Average Grade - 4.9% (9%)	Rating - 2.25 (cat 1)

Take Old Siskiyou Highway up toward the Mount Ashland Ski Area. After 3.5 miles it goes through a unique 270 degree turn. At mile 6.7 cross under I-5 and turn left at the stop sign. After a half mile turn right toward Mount Ashland Ski Area. After passing the Mount Ashland Inn you soon reach the Mount Ashland Ski Area. The climb ends just beyond the ski area.

Directions - From the junction of I-5 and route 66 in Ashland, OR head east on 66 for ~5 miles to Old Siskiyou Highway (right). The climb begins at the junction.

Facilities - Medford, OR   Airport - Medford, OR

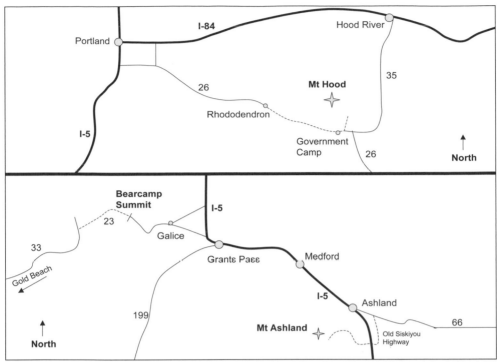

Mt. Hood, Bear Camp Summit West and Mt. Ashland, OR

Approaching the top of Mt. Ashland in Oregon

Utah

Guardsman Pass

Total elevation - 4,814 ft	Length - 17.1 miles
Average Grade - 5.3% (11%)	Rating - 3.01 (hors/cat 1)

This climb may be the most difficult in Utah up very scenic Cottonwood Canyon (190) on a route that does carry some traffic. Look for steeper ramps near the top before the finish at Guardsman Pass (closed in winter - Wasatch-Cache National Forest - 801 733-2660).

Directions - From I-215 in Salt Lake City head east. Take exit 7 and go south on Wasatch Blvd to its intersection with route 190. The climb begins at the junction by heading up 190.

Facilities - Salt Lake City, UT   Airport - Salt Lake City, UT

Little Cottonwood Canyon

Total elevation - 3,365 ft	Length - 8.8 miles
Average Grade - 7.2% (10%)	Rating - 2.79 (hors/cat 1)

Little Cottonwood is a very difficult and scenic climb into the Wasatch Mountains within a steep walled canyon. The ride ends just above the Alta ski resort where the pavement turns to dirt. This one is a very fast descent.

Directions - From I-15 in Sandy, UT head east on route 209 to its junction with route 210 at the mouth of Little Cottonwood Canyon. The climb begins there by continuing east on 210.

Facilities - Salt Lake City, UT   Airport - Salt Lake City, UT

Alpine Summit (east)

Total elevation - 2,836 ft	Length - 8.7 miles
Average Grade - 6.2% (10%)	Rating - 1.96 (cat 1)

The east side of Alpine Summit (route 92) is a stout and scenic climb past the Sundance Resort. The road gets very tight and twisty and passes through the largest grove of Aspens the author as ever seen. The climb ends at an unmarked pass (closed in winter - Uinta National Forest - 801 785-3563). The west side is also a nice climb (10.7 miles at 5.3%).

Directions - From Orem, UT head up route 189 toward Heber. After 6.8 miles route 92 will appear (suddenly) on the left. The climb begins at the junction.

Facilities - Orem, UT   Airport - Salt Lake City, UT

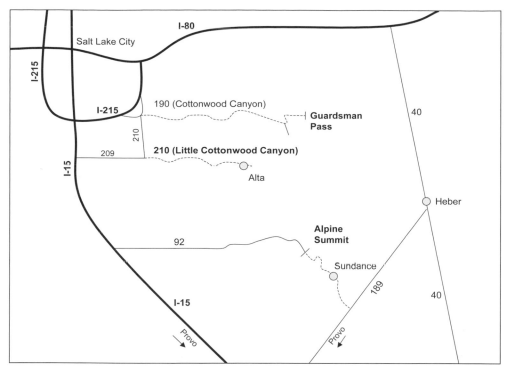

Guardsman Pass West, Little Cottonwood Canyon and Alpine Summit East, UT

A scene along very tough Little Cottonwood Canyon

Nebo Loop Road (north)

Total elevation - 3,753 ft	Length - 15.0 miles
Average Grade - 4.7% (9%)	Rating - 2.02 (cat 1)

The north side of Nebo Loop Rd is a fairly shallow but scenic climb. The climb ends at an unmarked summit (if you reach Utah Lake overlook (right) you have passed the listed summit). The road continues but true climbing has ended (closed in winter – Uinta National Forest - 801 785-3563). The south side is also is a solid climb (~3,200 ft over ~13 miles).

Directions - From I-15 in Payson, UT take exit 252 and head east on 800 south for 1.3 miles to Payson Canyon Rd (right). Head up Payson Canyon Rd for 7/10ths mile to its intersection with 600 East where the climb begins by continuing south on Payson Canyon Rd.

Facilities - Provo, UT   **Airport** - Salt Lake City, UT

31 (west)

Total Elevation - 3,795 ft	Length - 13.2 miles
Average Grade - 5.5% (10%)	Rating - 2.43 (cat 1)

Route 31 is an interesting and isolated climb up into the high country of central Utah along a very stout grade over the first 2/3rds of the hill. The climb ends (9785 ft) at the intersection with Skyline Drive (signed dirt road on the right) in an alpine setting. The east side of 31 is a very long and shallow climb up to Skyline Drive (~3,700 ft of climbing over twenty-six miles).

Directions - In Fairview, UT the climb begins at the intersection of routes 31 and 89.

Facilities - Provo, UT   **Airport** - Salt Lake City, UT

Castle Valley

Total elevation - 3,518 ft	Length - 13.5 miles
Average Grade - 4.9% (10%)	Rating - 1.92 (cat 1)

Castle Valley begins at the Colorado River along one of the most spectacular roads in the U.S. After 10.6 miles turn right on La Sal Mountain Road. This section is steeper with views of the surrounding mountains. The climb ends after 13.5 miles at a 180 degree bend over a saddle (unmarked). The road continues but true climbing has ended.

Directions - From Moab, UT head north on scenic route 128 for 15.2 miles to Castle Valley Rd on the right where the climb begins.

Facilities - Moab, UT   **Airport** - Grand Junction, CO

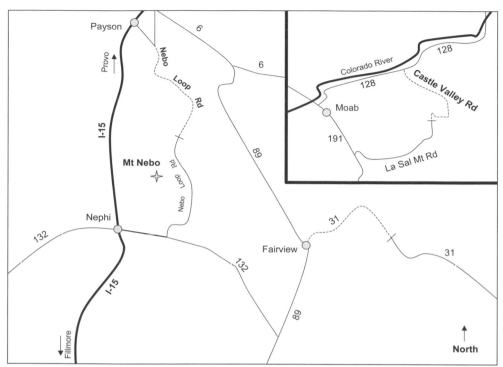

Nebo Loop Rd North, 31 West and Castle Valley, UT

Near the bottom of very scenic Castle Valley in Utah

153/Elk Meadows

Total elevation - 4,266 ft

Average Grade - 4.5% (11%)

Length - 17.8 miles

Rating - 2.31 (cat 1)

The route up 153 to Elk Meadows is a solid climb to high altitude. The road heads up a drainage along a creek over the bottom half of the climb. After a few scenic switchbacks the high mountains appear and you enter a small valley where the grade flattens. You soon pass the Elk Meadows ski area (right) where the grade increases. At mile 16.6 turn left on an unmarked road. This last stretch is steep and ends at a parking lot at over 10,000 ft.

Directions - From Main Street in Beaver, UT head east on Route 153 for 2.2 miles. You will have just made a 90 degree turn to the left and a golf course is on your left. The climb begins here by heading up the hill.

Facilities - Cedar City, UT

Airport - Las Vegas, NV

153

Total elevation - 3,929 ft

Average Grade - 4.2% (10%)

Length - 17.7 miles

Rating - 1.94 (cat 1)

Identical to the previous climb except you stay on route 153 to its unmarked summit. This last section is more shallow than the finishing stretch to Elk Meadows.

Directions - From Main Street in Beaver, UT head east on Route 153 for 2.2 miles. You will have just made a 90 degree turn and a golf course is on your left. The climb begins here.

Facilities - Cedar City, UT

Airport - Las Vegas, NV

143 (north)

Total elevation - 4,339 ft

Average Grade - 5.9% (12%)

Length - 13.9 miles

Rating - 3.07 (hors/cat 1)

This climb is another contender for the most difficult in Utah. The first nine miles are along a slowly increasing grade then there is a steep section through hairpin turns. At mile 11 you pass through the town of Brian Head, UT. Leaving town the grade increases again before easing just before the signed summit (10,420 ft).

Directions - From I-15 in Parowan, UT head south on Route 143 through town. The climb begins at the edge of Parowan at the corner of 143 and City View Drive.

Facilities - Cedar City, UT

Airport - Las Vegas, NV

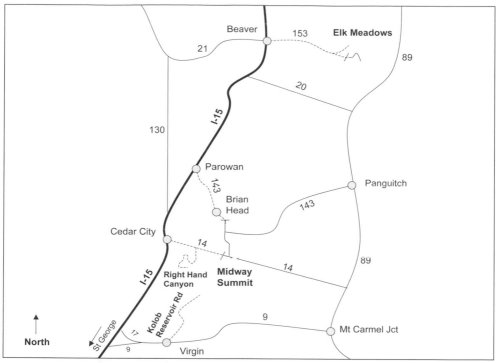

153/Elk Meadows, 153 and 143 North, UT

A big switchback along the difficult climb up route 143 in Utah

Cedar Canyon

Total elevation - 3,904 ft	Length - 16.6 miles
Average Grade - 4.5% (10%)	Rating - 2.05 (cat 1)

Cedar Canyon is a very scenic climb that follows a drainage up toward Cedar Breaks National Monument. The grade increases over the second half of the climb before ending at unmarked (as of 2006) Midway Summit (9,896 ft).
Directions - From I-15 in Cedar City, UT head east on route 14. Near the east edge of town and just before Highland Rd there is a bridge over a creek where the climb begins.

Facilities - Cedar City, UT   Airport - Las Vegas, NV

Right Hand Canyon

Total elevation - 3,228 ft	Length - 12.1 miles
Average Grade - 5.1% (10%)	Rating - 1.88 (cat 1)

This climb shares its start with Cedar Canyon. After 4.4 miles turn right on Right Hand Canyon Rd. The road twists up the mountain and eventually heads up a ridge with great views. It eventually heads back into the trees and the climb ends a short distance before the road turns to dirt.
Directions - From I-15 in Cedar City, UT head east on route 14. Near the east edge of town and just before Highland Rd there is a bridge over a creek where the climb begins.

Facilities - Cedar City, UT   Airport - Las Vegas, NV

Kolob Reservoir Road

Total elevation - 4,150 ft	Length - 14.9 miles
Average Grade - 5.3% (10%)	Rating - 2.45 (cat 1)

This is a very scenic climb that leads into Zion National Park along a variable grade. The climb continues beyond Wildcat Canyon trailhead and ends at an aspen grove (unmarked) at mile 14.9. The road continues but without any additional significant climbing and eventually turns to dirt.

Directions - The climb begins by getting to the junction of Route 9 and Kolob Reservoir Rd in the small town of Virgin, UT. Head up Kolob Reservoir Rd for 4.4 miles (to the bridge over North Creek) where the climb begins.

Facilities - Springdale, UT   Airport - Las Vegas, NV

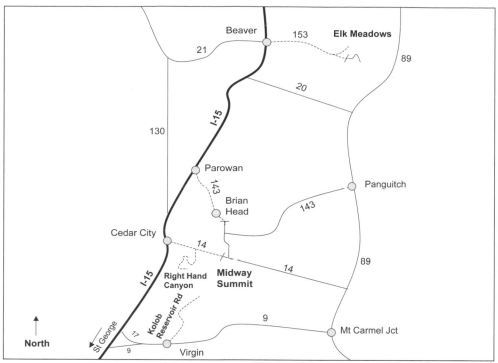

Cedar Canyon, Right Hand Canyon and Kolob Reservoir Rd, UT

The very scenic Kolob Reservoir Rd in Utah

Washington

Hurricane Ridge

Total elevation - 5,020 ft   Length - 18.2 miles

Average Grade - 5.2% (9%)   Rating - 2.71 (cat 1)

The most difficult climb in Washington, Hurricane Ridge is a scenic ride into Olympic National Park along a very consistent grade. After 3/10ths mile you will pass a visitors center on the right. Soon great views appear on your left. Pass through three short tunnels one right after another on the way up. Near the top the trees part to reveal amazing views of snow capped peaks on clear days. The climb ends at the upper park visitor's center on the left at 5,242 ft (the road continues for a short distance but descends). There is often weather in this area but the road is open all year (plowed in winter). Make sure you carry cold/wet weather gear at all times on this one.

Directions - The climb begins at the intersection of Race Street and Lauridsen Boulevard in scenic Port Angeles, WA. From the intersection, follow the signs toward Olympic National Park.

Facilities - Port Angeles, WA   **Airport** - Seattle, WA

Mount Spokane

Total elevation - 3,828 ft   Length - 13.1 miles

Average Grade - 5.5% (10%)   Rating - 2.23 (cat 1)

Mount Spokane is a great climb up into the mountains of eastern Washington. The grade increases once you enter Mount Spokane State Park with ~7 miles to left to the summit. The above stats for this climb are estimates and reports from others. The road ends just before the actual mountain top (closed in winter - Mount Spokane State Park - 509 238-4258). This climb is often used in area races.

Directions - From the small town of Mead, WA which is just north of Spokane, head east on route 206. The climb begins after approximately six miles.

Facilities - Spokane, WA   **Airport** - Spokane, WA

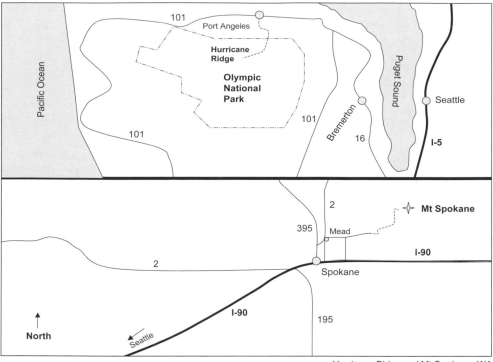

Hurricane Ridge and Mt Spokane, WA

The views approaching the top of Hurricane Ridge within Olympic National Park

Wyoming

Powder River Pass (west)

Total elevation - 4,942 ft

Length - 25.4 miles

Average Grade - 3.7% (8%)

Rating - 2.14 (cat 1)

This is a long and shallow climb up to high altitude in the Big Horn Mountains of Wyoming. The hill begins by following route 16 through scenic Ten Sleep Creek canyon. Soon you ascend a big s-curve up the ridge and out of the canyon. The climb flattens out over the last 9 miles to finish at the unmarked (as of 9/02) Powder River Pass (9,666 ft). The east side is a long, shallow climb (~4,900 ft over ~34 miles) with many descents along the way that begins in Buffalo, WY.

Directions - From the small town of Ten Sleep, WY head east on route 16 for 3.4 miles (just beyond its junction with route 436 on the right). The climb begins as route 16 dips just after the junction.

Facilities - Sheridan, WY

Airport - Casper, WY

Granite Pass (west)

Total elevation - 4,354 ft

Length - 16.5 miles

Average Grade - 5.0% (10%)

Rating - 2.50 (cat 1)

From route 14 within scenic Shell Creek Canyon, the climb begins by heading out of the canyon on a stout grade. After a decrease, the grade increases again at mile 5.2 as you cross the creek. Several miles later there is small descent and from that point the grade is fairly shallow over the finishing stretch through high mountain meadows as you top out at Granite Pass (9,033 ft).

Directions - In the tiny town of Shell, WY head east on route 14 into Shell Creek Canyon for almost 6 miles. The climb begins as the road increases in grade as it heads up the right side of the canyon.

Facilities - Cody, WY

Airport - Billings, MT

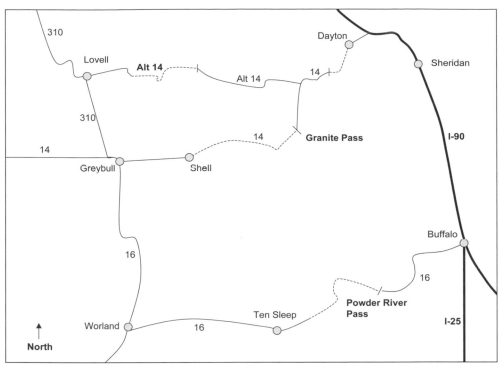

Powder River Pass West and Granite Pass West, WY

Looking back down Granite Pass West in WY

14 (east)

Total elevation - 3,934 ft	Length - 14.9 miles
Average Grade - 5.0% (10%)	Rating - 2.19 (cat 1)

This climb heads up a red colored road towards the Big Horn Mountains of Wyoming. Around five miles into climb the grade increases as you start to switchback up the hill with great views down into the valley. It ends after 14.9 miles at an unmarked top. You can continue to ride another 11.2 mostly flat miles to Burgess Junction and then go left for another 9.8 miles to reach Granite Pass (see Granite Pass west) but any significant climbing has ended.

Directions - This climb begins by heading west on route 14 at the western edge of the small town of Dayton, WY.

Facilities - Sheridan, WY   **Airport** - Billings, MT

Alternate 14

Total elevation - 5,315 ft	Length - 18.6 miles
Average Grade - 5.4% (11%)	Rating - 3.34 (hors/cat 1)

The hardest climb in Wyoming, the route starts out on a shallow, steady grade. For the first few miles the road is very straight and you can clearly see your objective ahead. After 6.4 miles the grade increases as you start to switchback up the hill. Eventually the road clings to the side of a cliff with great views. After entering a gorge, the grade eases, there is a small descent, climbing resumes and then the climb ends (unmarked) at a brake check area for cars which is on your left as you ascend. After a small descent the road continues to gain in elevation but significant climbing has ended. The lower half of this route will be very hot in the afternoons in summer as it faces west and is exposed all the way (closed in winter - Bighorn National Forest - 307 674-2600).

Directions - From Lovell, WY head east on Alternate Route 14. Once you cross the Big Horn River continue 2.3 miles to the Yellowtail Wildlife Habitat Management Area on the right where you can park. The climb starts just beyond the parking area at the bridge over a normally dry wash.

Facilities - Cody, WY   **Airport** - Billings, MT

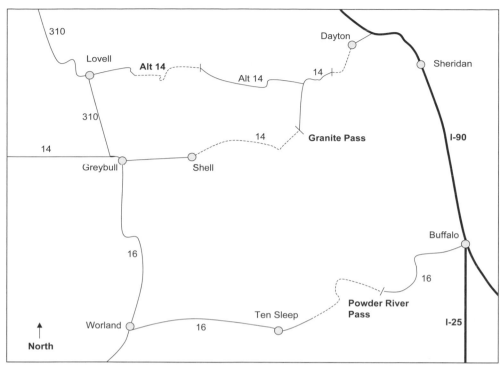

14 East and Alternate 14, WY

A warning sign near the top of Alternate 14 in Wyoming

Teton Pass (east)

Total elevation - 2,287 ft	Length - 5.5 miles
Average Grade - 7.9% (12%)	Rating - 1.92 (cat 1)

Teton Pass (8,429 ft) is a very stout and scenic climb along route 22 west of Jackson, WY. There is an alternate climb along old route 22 that parallels route 22. It is a bit more up and down but scenic and cars are not allowed. The west side of Teton Pass is a very shallow climb and not worth the effort (if you are looking for serious climbing).

Directions - The climb begins on route 22 at the western city limit of the small town of Wilson, WY.

Facilities - Jackson, WY	**Airport** - Jackson, WY

Beartooth Pass (east)

Total elevation - 5,272 ft	Length - 30.4 miles
Average Grade - 3.3% (8%)	Rating - 2.10 (cat 1)

Included due to its finishing height and scenery, this is a long climb into the Beartooth Mountains. Never very steep but with amazing views down into the valley as you ascend multiple switchbacks. At mile 22 the climb pops out above treeline and heads across alpine terrain. At mile 27 there is a descent before the final push up to Beartooth Pass at 10,947 ft (closed in winter - Shoshone National Forest - 307 527-6241). The west side of Beartooth Pass is also a scenic but shallow climb (19.7 miles at 3.7%).

Directions - The climb begins in Red Lodge, MT by heading west on Route 212 from the junction of routes 212 and 308.

Facilities - Billings, MT	**Airport** - Billings, MT

Snowy Range Pass (east)

Total elevation - 2,787 ft	Length - 8.5 miles
Average Grade - 6.2% (10%)	Rating - 2.09 (cat 1)

A scenic and stout high altitude climb up to Snowy Range Pass (10,847 ft) in the Rockies. The west side is a very long and shallow climb from the North Platte River (closed in winter - Medicine Bow National Forest - 307 745-2300).

Directions - The climb begins in Centennial, WY by heading west on route 130.

Facilities - Laramie, WY	**Airport** - Denver, CO

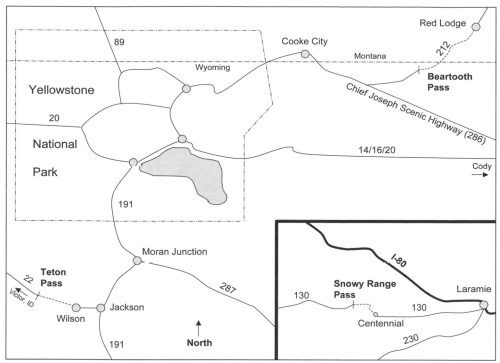

Teton Pass West, Beartooth Pass East and Snowy Range Pass West, WY

A scenic section and drop off along the road to Beartooth Pass

Selected Hill Climb Races

East

Mount Washington Hill Climb (NH) - The most difficult hill climb race in the U.S. and perhaps the world, the Mount Washington Hill Climb takes place each August (see climb description). For details go to www.tinmtn.org/hillclimb.

Mount Auscutney Hill Climb (VT) - Ride one of the steepest roads in the U.S. (see climb description). For details go to www.bikereg.com.

Gear Up for Lyme Mount Equinox Hill Climb (VT) - A very difficult race up Mt. Equinox and currently the only legal way to ride the hill (see climb description). For details go to www. gearupforlyme.com.

Whiteface Mountain (NY) - A great climb up a tough hill (see climb description). For details go to www.whitefacerace.com.

Mount Greylock Hill Climb (MA) - This race climbs the north site of Mount Greylock (see climb description). It is usually run in Sept/Oct with the date being set about one month before the event. Call The Spoke bike shop in Williamstown, MA for information at (413) 458-3456.

West

Mount Tamalpais Hill Climb (CA) - Possibly the second oldest hill climb race in the U.S. up beautiful Mount Tamalpais just north of San Francisco, CA. For details go to www. californiaroadclub.org.

Bob Cook Memorial Mount Evans Hill Climb (CO) - The oldest hill climb race in the U.S. is usually held in late July (see climb description). Go to www.bicyclerace.com.

Lookout Mountain Hill Climb (CO) - Not a difficult climb but a local favorite. Many Colorado cyclists know their best time from 'pillar to post' up this hill. Currently part of the Oredigger Classic. Go to www.mines.edu/Stu_life/organ/bike/racing.html.

Taos Mountain Hill Climb (NM) - A climb up Taos Ski Mountain usually held in August. For details go to www.alpineclassic.org.

Santa Fe Hill Climb (NM) - This hill climb race follows the total length of route 475 out of Santa Fe up to the ski resort. Go to www.nmcycling.com.

Mount Graham Hill Climb (AZ) - Almost the full paved length of Mount Graham is used making this is one of the toughest hill climb races in the U.S. (see climb description). For details go to www.presteza.homstead.com/MtGrahamIndex~ns4.html.

Mount Lemmon Hill Climb (AZ) - This race only tackles about 1/3 the length of massive Mount Lemmon but is still a tough climb (see climb description). For details go to www. azcycling.com.

Snowbowl Hill Climb (AZ) - A short and scenic hill climb up to the Snowbowl Ski Area on the slopes of Humphreys Peak near Flagstaff, AZ. For details go to www.azcycling.com.

Kitt Peak Hill Climb (AZ) - A tough climb up to the observatories at Kitt Peak, west of Tucson, AZ (see climb description). For details go to www.azcycling.com.

Western Montana Hill Climb Championships (MT) - An annual climbing event in Montana. For details go to www.montanacycling.org.

Mount Charleston Hill Climb (NV) - A very competitive and difficult climb up massive route 156 just outside of Las Vegas, NV (see climb description). For details check out any major bike shop in Las Vegas.

Snowbird Hill Climb (UT) - This tough hill climb race heads up Little Cottonwood Canyon to the ski resort of Alta (see climb description). For details go to www.sports-am.com.

Porcupine Big Cottonwood Hill Climb (UT) - A racing climb that funds cancer research, the route is up Cottonwood Canyon just southeast of Salt Lake City, UT (see climb description). Details at www.cycleutah.com.

Sundance Hill Climb (UT) - This hill climb race near Provo, UT goes by the Sundance Ski resort on route 92 through one of the largest aspen groves around (see climb description). Go to www.cycleutah.com.

Teton Pass Hill Climb (WY) - A tough climbing race up stout Teton Pass in Wyoming (see climb description). For details go to www.ucjh.org.

The top of tough Sonora Pass, CA

Organized Races/Rides with Significant Climbing
(in order of climbing to mileage)

Sand Dunes to Sierras Stage Race (CA) - 13,425 miles of climbing over ~70 miles. For details go to www.everestchallenge.com.

Everest Challenge (CA) - 29,035 ft of climbing (Everest, get it?) over 206 miles. For details go to www.everestchallenge.com.

Blood, Sweat and Gears (NC) - > 13,000 feet of climbing over 100 miles through the mountains of northern North Carolina. For details go to www.bloodsweatandgears.org.

Brasstown Bald Buster Century (GA) - > 12,000 feet of climbing over 100 miles through north Georgia and some of the same terrain that the annual Tour de Georgia covers. For details go to www.brasstownbaldbustercentury.com.

Death Ride (CA) - A very difficult ride with > 15,000 ft of climbing over 129 miles. For details go to www.deathride.com.

Mount Shasta Summit Century (CA) - 15,500 ft of climbing over 135 miles. For details go to www.shastahom.com/summit-century.

Three Mountain Metric (NC) - 8,600 feet of climbing over 75 miles in North Carolina including the very tough climb up Pilot Mountain (2.2 miles at 8.9%). For details go to www.home.triad.rr.com/threemtnmetric/.

Assault on Mount Mitchell (NC) - 11,000 ft of climbing over 100 miles that ends at the top of Mount Mitchell. For details go to www.freewheelers.info/assaultl.html.

Six Gap Century (GA) - 10,700 ft of climbing over 100 miles through north Georgia. For details go to www.dahlonega.org/sixgapcentury/index.html.

Auburn Century (CA) - 11,000 feet of climbing over 106 miles through the Sierra foothills. For details go to www.auburncentury.com.

Tour de Cashiers (NC) - 10,500 of climbing over 101 miles through scenic western North Carolina. For details go to www.tourdecashiers.com.

Devil Mountain Double Century (CA) - 20,000 ft of climbing in 200 miles. For details go to www.bbcnet.com/devilmountain/devilmountain.asp.

The Mountain Mama Road Bike Challenge (VA) - 10,000 feet of climbing over 100 miles through the scenic but surprising tough Allegheny Mountains of Virginia. For details go to: http://bikemountainmama.homestead.com.

100 Most Difficult Road Bike Climbs in the U.S.
(Author Rating; Major Tour Rating)

1. Mt. Washington, NH	(6.45; hors)	51. Rose Summit North, NV	(2.55; cat 1)
2. Mauna Loa, HI	(6.33; hors)	52. Cold Springs Summit, CA	(2.55; cat 1)
3. Haleakala, HI	(6.13; hors)	53. Emigrant Pass East, CA	(2.54; cat 1)
4. Mauna Kea, HI	(5.26; hors)*, **	54. Valley of the Falls, CA	(2.53; cat 1)
5. Onion Valley, CA	(4.68; hors)	55. Bearcamp Summit West, OR	(2.50; cat 1)
6. Horseshoe Meadows, CA	(4.58; hors)	56. Mt. Charleston, NV	(2.50; cat 1)
7. White Mtn, CA	(4.31; hors)***	57. Granite Pass West, WY	(2.50; cat 1)
8. Sherman Pass West, CA	(4.06; hors)****	58. Grand Mesa South, CO	(2.50; cat 1)
9. Whitney Portal, CA,	(3.98; hors)	59. 18 South, CA	(2.50; cat 1)
10. Mt. Evans, CO	(3.88; hors)	60. Dantes View, CA	(2.50; cat 1)
11. Mt. Equinox, VT	(3.79; hors)	61. Baldwin/Olinda, HI	(2.48; cat 1)
12. Mt. Graham, AZ	(3.64; hors)	62. Burke Mtn, VT	(2.47; cat 1)
13. Mt. Baldy, CA	(3.57; hors)	63. Daylight Pass Long, CA	(2.47; cat 1)
14. 156, NV	(3.57; hors)	64. 18 North, CA	(2.45; cat 1)
15. Shirley Meadows East, CA	(3.57; hors)	65. Kolob Reservoir Rd, UT	(2.45; cat 1)
16. South Lake, CA	(3.52; hors)	66. Sandia Crest, NM	(2.44; cat 1)
17. Palomar Mtn, CA	(3.43; hors)	67. Death Valley Rd East, CA	(2.43; cat 1)
18. Grand Mesa North, CO	(3.39; hors/cat 1)	68. 31 West, UT	(2.43; cat 1)
19. Wheeler Peak, NV	(3.39; hors/cat 1)	69. Townes Pass West, CA	(2.40; cat 1)
20. Rock Creek Rd, CA	(3.38; hors/cat 1)	70. Gilbraltor Rd, CA	(2.40; cat 1)
21. Alternate 14, WY	(3.34; hors/cat 1)	71. 39/Crystal Lake, CA	(2.39; cat 1)
22. 190, CA	(3.32; hors/cat 1)	72. 138/Table Mtn, CA	(2.38; cat 1)
23. 156/158, NV	(3.32; hors/cat 1)	73. Monitor Pass East, CA	(2.38; cat 1)
24. Sequoia, CA	(3.19; hors/cat 1)	74. Independence Pass West, CO	(2.37; cat 1)
25. Lake Sabrina, CA	(3.15; hors/cat 1)	75. Cloudcroft, NM	(2.37; cat 1)
26. Whiteface Mtn, NY	(3.13; hors/cat 1)^	76. Okemo Mtn, VT	(2.36; cat 1)
27. 143 North, UT	(3.07; hors/cat 1)	77. Clingmans Dome West, NC	(2.34; cat 1)
28. Townes Pass East, CA	(3.04; hors/cat 1)	78. N4/Table Mtn, CA	(2.33; cat 1)
29. 157/158, NV	(3.04; hors/cat 1)	79. 153/Elk Meadows, UT	(2.31; cat 1)
30. Glacier Lodge, CA	(3.02; hors/cat 1)	80. 138/Blue Ridge Summit, CA	(2.30; cat 1)
31. Guardsman Pass, UT	(3.01; hors/cat 1)	81. Pine Creek, CA	(2.29; cat 1)
32. 330, CA	(2.97; hors/cat 1)	82. Figueroa Mtn Rd East, CA	(2.29; cat 1)
33. Mt. Lemmon, AZ	(2.97; hors/cat 1)	83. Mt. Ashland, OR	(2.25; cat 1)
34. Sonora Pass West, CA	(2.86; hors/cat 1)	84. Mt. Mitchell, NC	(2.24; cat 1)
35. Mt. Shasta, CA	(2.85; hors/cat 1)	85. N4/Blue Ridge Summit, CA	(2.24; cat 1)
36. Trail Ridge East, CO	(2.83; hors/cat 1)	86. Emigrant Pass West, CA	(2.23; cat 1)
37. Little Cottonwood Cyn, UT	(2.79; hors/cat 1)	87. Mt. Spokane, WA	(2.23; cat 1)
38. Nine Mile Grade, CA	(2.75; hors/cat 1)	88. 245/180, CA	(2.22; cat 1)
39. Mt. Auscutney, VT	(2.74; hors/cat 1)	89. Cottonwood Pass, CO	(2.20; cat 1)
40. Wildrose, CA	(2.73; cat 1)	90. San Marcos/Painted Cave Rd, CA	(2.20; cat 1)
41. Hurricane Ridge, WA	(2.71; cat 1)	91. Shirley Meadows West, CA	(2.20; cat 1)
42. 180, CA	(2.68; cat 1)	92. 14 East, WY	(2.19; cat 1)
43. 168 West, CA	(2.68; cat 1)	93. Hicks/Mt. Umunhum, CA	(2.18; cat 1)
44. J21/245/180, CA	(2.66; cat 1)	94. Kings Canyon, CA	(2.14; cat 1)
45. Mt. Hood, OR	(2.65; cat 1)	95. Brasstown Bald, GA	(2.14; cat 1)
46. Mineral King, CA	(2.63; cat 1)	96. Alba Rd, CA	(2.14; cat 1)
47. Tollhouse Rd/168, CA	(2.63; cat 1)	97. Powder River Pass West, WY	(2.14; cat 1)
48. Daylight Pass, CA	(2.60; cat 1)	98. Roan Mtn North, NC	(2.13; cat 1)
49. East Portal, CO	(2.60; cat 1)	99. 39, CA	(2.12; cat 1)
50. Stainback Rd, HI	(2.58; cat 1)	100. Kitt Peak, AZ	(2.11; cat 1)

* Stelvio Pass East, Italy (15.3 miles at 7.3%)   **Mortirolo, Italy (7.7 miles at 10.6%)

Angliru, Spain (7.8 miles at 10.1%)   * Mt Ventoux, France (13.3 miles at 7.5%)

^ L'Alpe d'Huez, France (8.1 miles at 8.4%)

100 Toughest USA Road Bike Climbs
(without adjusting for altitude)*

1. Mt. Washington, NH
2. Mauna Loa, HI
3. Haleakala, HI
4. Mauna Kea, HI
5. Onion Valley, CA
6. Horseshoe Meadows, CA
7. Mt. Equinox, VT
8. White Mtn, CA
9. Sherman Pass West, CA,
10. Whitney Portal, CA
11. Mt. Baldy, CA
12. Shirley Meadows East, CA
13. Palomar Mtn, CA
14. Mt. Graham, AZ
15. 156, NV
16. Whiteface Mtn, NY
17. 190, CA
18. Sequoia, CA
19. South Lake, CA
20. Mt. Evans, CO
21. Townes Pass East, CA
22. 156/158, NV
23. Alternate 14, WY
24. Wheeler Peak, NV
25. Rock Creek Rd, CA
26. 330, CA
27. Grand Mesa North, CO
28. Lake Sabrina, CA
29. Glacier Lodge Rd, CA
30. 157/158, NV
31. Mt. Auscutney, VT
32. Hurricane Ridge, WA
33. Wildrose, CA
34. Nine Mile Grade, CA
35. Mt. Lemmon, AZ
36. 168, CA
37. Guardsman Pass, UT
38. 143, UT
39. Mt. Shasta, CA
40. Tollhouse Rd/168, CA
41. Daylight Pass, CA
42. Sonora Pass West, CA
43. Mt. Hood, OR
44. 180 West, CA
45. Mineral King Rd, CA
46. J21/245/180, CA
47. Emigrant Pass East, CA
48. Bear Camp Summit West, OR
49. Little Cottonwood Canyon, UT
50. Burke Mtn Rd, VT

51. Baldwin/Olinda, HI
52. Daylight Pass Long, CA
53. Dantes View, CA
54. 180, CA
55. 18 South, CA
56. Valley of the Falls, CA
57. Gilbraltor Rd, CA
58. Townes Pass West, CA
59. Okemo Mtn, VT
60. Cold Springs Summit, CA
61. East Portal, CO
62. 39/Crystal Lake, CA
63. 18 North, CA
64. Trail Ridge Pass, CO
65. Mt. Charleston, NV
66. Figueroa Mtn Rd East, CA
67. Rose Summit East, NV
68. Hicks/Mt. Umunhum, CA
69. Clingmans Dome West, NC
70. Death Valley Rd East, CA
71. Kolob Reservoir Rd, UT
72. San Marcos/Painted Cave Rd, CA
73. Granite Pass West, WY
74. 138/Table Mtn, CA
75. Emigrant Pass West, CA
76. Alba Rd, CA
77. N4/Table Mtn, CA
78. Mt. Spokane, WA
79. Monitor Pass East, CA
80. Mt. Ashland, OR
81. 138/Blue Ridge Summit, CA
82. Brasstown Bald, GA
83. Cloudcroft, NM
84. 245/180, CA
85. Mt. Mitchell, NC
86. 31 West, UT
87. Grand Mesa South, CO
88. Pine Creek Rd, CA
89. Bohlman/On Orbit, CA
90. Old Priest Grade, CA
91. N4/Blue Ridge Summit, CA
92. Shirley Meadows West, CA
93. 39, CA
94. Sandia Crest, NM
95. Bohlman Rd, CA
96. Roan Mtn North, TN/NC
97. Kings Canyon, CA
98. 14 East, WY
99. Kitt Peak, AZ
100. Figueroa Mtn Rd West, CA

* All climbs described in text

Most Difficult Climbing Sections*

1/10 Mile:
1. Canton Avenue, Pittsburgh, PA - 35%
2. Fargo St (between Allesandro and N. Alvarado), Los Angeles, CA - 32.5%
3. Eldred St, Los Angeles, CA - 32%
4. Filbert St (between Hyde and Leavenworth), San Francisco, CA - 31.5%
5. 22nd St (between Church and Vicksburg), San Francisco, CA - 31%

Half Mile:
1. Kingsley Hill Road, Monroe Bridge, MA (mile 0.0-0.5) - 19.2%
2. Marin Avenue, Berkeley, CA (mile 1.75-2.25) - 18.1%
3. Lincoln Gap East, VT (mile 0.9-1.4) - 16.3%
4. Old Priest Grade, CA (mile 0.3-0.8) - 15.9%
5. Lincoln Gap West, VT (mile 0.0-0.5) - 15.8%

Mile:
1. Lincoln Gap East, VT (mile 0.5-1.5) - 15.9%
2. Marin Avenue, Berkeley, CA (mile 1.5-2.5) - 14.1%
3. Old Priest Grade, CA (mile 0.3 - 1.3) - 15.0%
4. Burke Mountain, VT (mile 0.0-1.0) - 14.8%
5. Bohlman Road/On Orbit Drive, CA (mile 1.1-2.1) - 14.6%

5 Miles:
1. Mt. Washington, NH (first 5 miles) - 12.1%
2. Mt. Equinox, VT (last 5 miles) - 11.5%
3. Shirley Meadows East, CA (mile 1.9-6.9) - 9.6%
4. Whitney Portal, CA (mile 5.7-10.7) - 9.2%
5. Onion Valley Road, CA (mile 4.5-9.5) - 8.8%
6. Whiteface Mountain, NY (mile 1.2-6.2) - 8.9%
7. San Marcos/Painted Cave Road, CA (last 5 miles) - 8.7%
8. Mt. Baldy, CA (mile 7.6-12.6) - 8.5%
9. Townes Pass West, CA (mile 2.5-7.5) - 8.5%
10. Horseshoe Meadows, CA (mile 10.9-15.9) - 8.1%

10 Miles:
1. Onion Valley Rd, CA (last 10 miles) - 8.3%
2. Whitney Portal, CA (last 10 miles) - 8.0%
3. Horseshoe Meadows, CA (mile 5.9 -15.9) - 7.9%
4. Shirley Meadows East, CA (first 10 miles) - 7.8%
5. Mt. Baldy, CA (last 10 miles) - 7.6%
6. Sherman Pass West, CA (mile 5.1-14.1) - 7.1%
7. Glacier Lodge, CA (first 10 miles) - 7.1%
8. Palomar Mountain, CA (last 10 miles) - 7.3%
9. Nine Mile Grade, CA (first 10 miles) - 7.0%
10. Tollhouse Rd/168, CA (last 10 miles) - 6.9%

* Rankings are adjusted for altitude

Greatest Elevation Gained Climbs
(minimum 5,000 vertical feet)*

1.	Mauna Loa, HI -	11,091 ft (3380 meters)
2.	Haleakala, HI -	9,997 ft (3047 meters)
3.	Mauna Kea, HI -	9,117 ft (2779 meters)
4.	Mt. Evans, CO -	6,590 ft (2009 meters)
5.	Horseshoe Meadows, CA -	6,234 ft (1900 meters)
6.	Mt. Lemmon, AZ -	6,222 ft (1896 meters)
7.	White Mtn, CA -	6,204 ft (1891 meters)
8.	190, CA -	6,199 ft (1888 meters)
9.	J21/245/180, CA -	5,750 ft (1753 meters)
10.	Grand Mesa North, CO -	5,622 ft (1714 meters)
11.	157/158, NV -	5,621 ft (1709 meters)
12.	Mt. Graham, AZ -	5,572 ft (1698 meters)
13.	Rock Creek Rd, CA -	5,548 ft (1691 meters)
14.	Dantes View, CA -	5,475 ft (1669 meters)
15.	South Lake, CA -	5,445 ft (1660 meters)
16.	156, NV -	5,348 ft (1630 meters)
17.	Alternate 14, WY -	5,335 ft (1626 meters)
18.	Sherman Pass, CA -	5,316 ft (1620 meters)
19.	Emigrant Pass East, CA -	5,309 ft (1618 meters)
20.	Onion Valley, CA -	5,169 ft (1600 meters)
21.	180 West, CA -	5,163 ft (1574 meters)
22.	Mt. Mitchell, NC -	5,161 ft (1573 meters)
23.	Shirley Meadows West, CA -	5,133 ft (1564 meters)
24.	Sequoia, CA -	5,120 ft (1561 meters)
25.	Hurricane Ridge, WA -	5,020 ft (1530 meters)
26.	Mt. Charleston, NV -	5,020 ft (1530 meters)
27.	156/158 NV -	5,002 ft (1525 meters)

* All climbs described in the text. There are other routes that exceed 5,000 ft of elevation gain but they do not qualify as a climb either because the average grade is too shallow or a significant portion of their length is along flat and/or descending segments.

Highest Elevation Attained Roads*
(minimum 10,000 ft at climb summit)

1.	Mt. Evans, CO -	14,130 ft (4307 meters)*
2.	Trail Ridge, CO -	12,183 ft (3713 meters)*
3.	Cottonwood Pass, CO -	12,126 ft (3696 meters)*
4.	Independence Pass CO -	12,095 ft (3687 meters)*
5.	Loveland Pass, CO -	11,992 ft (3655 meters)*
6.	Hoosier Pass, CO -	11,541 ft (3518 meters)
7.	Slumgullion Pass, CO -	11,530 ft (3514 meters)*
8.	Fremont Pass, CO -	11,320 ft (3450 meters)
9.	Monarch Pass, CO -	11,312 ft (3448 meters)*
10.	Berthoud Pass, CO -	11,307 ft (3446 meters)
11.	Juniper Pass, CO -	11,130 ft (3392 meters)*
12.	Mauna Loa, HI -	11,115 ft (3388 meters)*
13.	Red Mtn Pass, CO -	11,081 ft (3358 meters)*
14.	Beartooth Pass, WY -	10,947 ft (3337 meters)*
15.	Molas Divide, CO -	10,910 ft (3322 meters)
16.	Spring Creek Pass, CO -	10,901 ft (3323 meters)
17.	Grand Mesa, CO -	10,852 ft (3308 meters)*
18.	Wolf Creek Pass, CO -	10,850 ft (3307 meters)
19.	Snowy Range Pass, WY -	10,847 ft (3306 meters)*
20.	Sandia Crest, NM -	10,661 ft (3249 meters)*
21.	Coal Bank Pass, CO -	10,640 ft (3243 meters)
22.	Mirror Lake Summit, UT -	10,600 ft (3231 meters)
23.	143, UT -	10,594 ft (3170 meters)
24.	64, NM -	10,507 ft (3202 meters)
25.	475, NM -	10,432 ft (3180 meters)
26.	Tennessee Pass, CO -	10,424 ft (3177 meters)
27.	153/Elk Meadows, UT -	10,342 ft (3152 meters)*
28.	Cameron Pass, CO -	10,276 ft (3132 meters)
29.	La Manga Pass, CO -	10,230 ft (3118 meters)
30.	Lizard Head Pass, CO -	10,222 ft (3116 meters)
31.	Rock Creek Rd, CA -	10,220 ft (3115 meters)*
32.	Wheeler Peak, NV -	10,163 ft (3098 meters)*
33.	White Mtn, CA -	10,152 ft (3094 meters)*
34.	North Pass, CO -	10,149 ft (3093 meters)
35.	Granella Pass Rd, CO -	10,105 ft (3080 meters)
36.	Horseshoe Meadows, CA -	10,034 ft (3058 meters)*
37.	Red Hill Pass, CO -	10,030 ft (3057 meters)
38.	Pikes Peak, CO	10,024 ft (3055 meters)*
39.	Haleakala, HI -	10,023 ft (3055 meters)*
40.	Cumbres Pass, CO -	10,022 ft (3055 meters)
41.	153, UT -	10,005 ft (3049 meters)*

* See climb description

Steepest Climbs (minimum 2.0 miles in length)

1. Burke Mountain, VT (13.4%)
2. Old Priest Grade, CA (13.1%)
3. Bohlman/On Orbit Dr, CA (12.8%)
4. Bohlman Rd, CA (12.0%)
5. Mt. Washington, NH (11.9%)
6. East Portal, CO (11.7%)
7. Mt. Equinox, VT (11.5%)
8. Mt. Auscutney, VT (11.5%)
9. Iowa Hill Rd East, CA (11.2%) - 2.0 miles long located just east of Colfax, CA.
10. Brasstown Bald, GA (11.1%)

Fastest Descents

1. 156, NV
2. Whiteface Mountain, NY
3. Lake Sabrina, CA
4. 156/158, NV
5. Townes Pass East, CA
6. Glacier Lodge Rd, CA
7. Daylight Pass, CA
8. Little Cottonwood Canyon, UT
9. Whitney Portal, CA
10. Dantes View, CA

Most Scenic/Spectacular Climbs (listed in guidebook)

1. Nacimiento Fergusson Rd, CA
2. Red Mountain Pass North, CO
3. Onion Valley, CA
4. Beartooth Pass East, MT/WY
5. Cherohala Skyway East, NC
6. Independence Pass West, CO
7. Horseshoe Meadows, CA
8. Castle Valley, UT
9. Whitney Portal, CA
10. Tioga Pass West, CA

Must Do Climbs - Listed alphabetically, these climbs are a mixture of the difficult, steep, and scenic. If you could only conquer 10 climbs in the U.S. I don't think too many would be disappointed with the following list.

- Brasstown Bald, GA
- Cherohala Skyway East, NC
- Mt. Evans, CO
- Mt. Graham, AZ
- Haleakala, HI
- Lincoln Gap East, VT
- Nacimiento Fergusson Rd, CA
- Onion Valley, CA
- Sonora Pass West, CA
- Mt. Washington, NH

King of the Mountains (KOM) Winners in Major Tours and U.S. Hill Climb Races

Tour de France:

1933 - Vincente Truba
1934 - Rene Vietto
1935 - Felicien Vervaecke
1936 - Julien Berrendero
1937 - Felicien Vervaecke
1938 - Gino Bartali
1939 - Sylvere Maes
1940 - Not held
1941 - Not held
1942 - Not held
1943 - Not held
1944 - Not held
1945 - Not held
1946 - Not held
1947 - Pierre Brambilla
1948 - Gino Bartali
1949 - Fauto Coppi
1950 - Louison Bobet
1951 - Raphael Germaniani
1952 - Fausto Coppi
1953 - Jesus Lorono
1954 - Federico Bahamontes
1955 - Charley Gaul
1956 - Charley Gaul
1957 - Gastone Nencini
1958 - Federico Bahamontes
1959 - Federico Bahamontes
1960 - Imerio Massignan
1961 - Imerio Massignan
1962 - Federico Bahamontes
1963 - Federico Bahamontes
1964 - Federico Bahamontes
1965 - Julio Jimenez
1966 - Julio Jimenez
1967 - Julio Jimenez
1968 - Aurellio Gonzalez
1969 - Eddy Merckx

1970 - Eddy Merkcx
1971 - Lucien Van Impe
1972 - Lucien Van Impe
1973 - Pedro Torres
1974 - Domingo Perurena
1975 - Lucien Van Impe
1976 - Giancario Bellini
1977 - Lucien Van Impe
1978 - Mario Martinez
1979 - Giovani Battaglin
1980 - Raymond Martin
1981 - Lucien Van Impe
1982 - Bernard Vallet
1983 - Lucien Van Impe
1984 - Robert Millar
1985 - Luis Herrera
1986 - Bernard Hinault
1987 - Luis Herrera
1988 - Steven Rooks
1989 - Gert Jan Theunisse
1990 - Thierry Clavevrolat
1991 - Claudio Chiappucci
1992 - Claudio Chiappucci
1993 - Tony Rominger
1994 - Richard Virenque
1995 - Richard Virenque
1996 - Richard Virenque
1997 - Richard Virenque
1998 - Christophe Rinero
1999 - Richard Virenque
2000 - Santiago Botero
2001 - Laurent Jalabert
2002 - Laurent Jalabert
2003 - Richard Virenque
2004 - Richard Virenque
2005 - Mickael Rasmussen
2006 - Mickael Rasmussen

Giro d'Italia:

1933 - Alfredo Binda
1934 - Remo Bertoni
1935 - Gino Bartali
1936 - Gino Bartali
1937 - Gino Bartali
1938 - Giovanni Valetti
1939 - Gino Bartali
1940 - Gino Bartali
1941 - Not held
1942 - Not held
1943 - Not held
1944 - Not held
1945 - Not held
1946 - Gino Bartali
1947 - Gino Bartali
1948 - Fausto Coppi
1949 - Fausto Coppi
1950 - Hugo Koblet
1951 - Louis Bobet
1952 - Raphael Geminiani
1953 - Pasquale Fornara
1954 - Fuasto Coppi
1955 - Gastone Nencini
1956 - *
1957 - Raphael Geminiani
1958 - Jean Brankart
1959 - Charley Gaul
1960 - Rik Van Looy
1961 - Vito Taccone
1962 - Angelino Soler
1963 - Vito Taccone
1964 - Franco Bitossi
1965 - Franco Bitossi
1966 - Franco Bitossi
1967 - Aurelio Gonzalez
1968 - Eddy Merkcx
1969 - Claudio Michelotto

1970 - Martin Vandenbossche
1971 - Manuel Fuente
1972 - Manuel Fuente
1973 - Manuel Fuente
1974 - Manuel Fuente
1975 - Francisco Galdos
1976 - Andres Oliva
1977 - Faustino Fernandez Ovies
1978 - Ueli Sutter
1979 - Claudio Bortolotto
1980 - Claudio Bortolotto
1981 - Claudio Bortolotto
1982 - Lucien Van Impe
1983 - Lucien Van Impe
1984 - Laurent Fignon
1985 - Jose Luis Navarro
1986 - Pedro Munoz
1987 - Robert Millar
1988 - Andy Hampsten
1989 - Luis Herrera
1990 - Claudio Chiappucci
1991 - Inaki Gaston
1992 - Claudio Chiappucci
1993 - Claudio Chiappucci
1994 - Pascal Richard
1995 - Mariano Piccoli
1996 - Mariano Piccoli
1997 - Jose Jaime Gonzales Pico
1998 - Marco Pantani
1999 - Jose Jaime Gonzales Pico
2000 - Francesco Casagrande
2001 - Jose Jaime Gonzales Pico
2002 - Julio Perez Cuapio
2003 - Jose Jaime Gonzales Pico
2004 - Fabian Wegmann
2005 - Jose Rujano
2006 - Juan Manuel Garate

* In 1956 the Giro awarded 3 KOM winners; one for each of 3 mountain sections used in that year's race (Federico Bahamontes, Charley Gaul & Cleto Maule).

Vuelta a Espana:

1935 - Eduardo Molinar
1936 - Salvador Molina
1937 - Not held
1938 - Not held
1939 - Not held
1940 - Not held
1941 - Fermin Trueba
1942 - Fermin Trueba
1943 - Not held
1944 - Not held
1945 - Julian Berrendero
1946 - Emilio Rodriguez
1947 - Emilio Rodriguez
1948 - Bernardo Ruiz
1949 - Not held
1950 - Emilio Rodriguez
1951 - Not held
1952 - Not held
1953 - Not held
1954 - Not held
1955 - Giuseppe Buratti
1956 - Nino Defillipis
1957 - Federico Bahamontes
1958 - Federico Bahamontes
1959 - Antonio Suarez
1960 - Antonio Karmany
1961 - Antonio Karmany
1962 - Antonio Karmany
1963 - Julio Jimenez
1964 - Julio Jimenez
1965 - Julio Jimenez
1966 - Gregorio San Miguel
1967 - Mariano Diaz
1968 - F. Gabicagogescoa
1969 - Luis Oscana
1970 - Augustin Tamames
1971 - Joop Zoetemelk

1972 - Jose Manuel Fuente
1973 - Jose Luis Abilleira
1974 - Jose Luis Abilleira
1975 - Andres Oliva
1976 - Andres Oliva
1977 - Pedro Torres
1978 - Andres Oliva
1979 - Felipe Yanaz
1980 - Juan Fernandez
1981 - Jose Luis Laguia
1982 - Jose Luis Laguia
1983 - Jose Luis Laguia
1984 - Felipe Yanaz
1985 - Jose Luis Laguia
1986 - Jose Luis Laguia
1987 - Luis Herrera
1988 - Alvaro Pino
1989 - Oscar Vargas
1990 - Martin Farfan
1991 - Luis Herrera
1992 - Carlos Hernandez
1993 - Toni Rominger
1994 - Luc Leblanc
1995 - Laurent Jalabert
1996 - Toni Rominger
1997 - Jose Maria Jimenez-Sastro
1998 - Jose Maria Jimenez-Sastro
1999 - Jose Maria Jimenez-Sastro
2000 - Carlos Sastre
2001 - Jose Maria Jimenez-Sastro
2002 - Keld Haagensen
2003 - Felix Cardenas
2004 - Felix Cardenas
2005 - Joaquin Rodriquez
2006 - Egoi Martinez

Mt Evans, Colorado:

1962 - S.Baillie/A.Weller (2:28)
1963 - Stuart Baillie (2:24)
1964 - Stuart Baillie (2:08:07)
1965 - Michael Hiltner (2:09:55)
1966 - Stuart Baillie (2:14)
1967 - No results
1968 - Mike Dennis (NA)
1969 - Stan Justice (2:19:23)
1970 - Kalman Halasi (2:22:49)
1971 - Kalman Halasi (2:14:35)
1972 - Bob Poling (2:11:41)
1973 - Jack Jenelle (2:05:32)
1974 - Jack Jenelle (2:05:09)
1975 - Bob Cook (2:02:55)
1976 - Bob Cook (1:57:50)
1977 - Bob Cook (1:55:43)
1978 - Bob Cook (1:54:27)
1979 - Not held
1980 - Bob Cook (1:54:56)
1981 - Alexi Grewal (1:57:36)
1982 - Don Spence (1:58:12)
1983 - Todd Gogulski (1:53:43)

1984 - Alexi Grewal (1:47:51)
1985 - Ned Overend (1:49:53)
1986 - Ned Overend (1:49:22)
1987 - Todd Gogulski (1:54:07)
1988 - Tom Resh (1:51:56)
1989 - Not held
1990 - Alexi Grewal (1:46:29)
1991 - Mike Engleman (1:51:41)
1992 - Mike Engleman (1:45:30)
1993 - Mike Engleman (1:56:57)
1994 - Mike Engleman (1:50:35)
1995 - Mike Engleman (1:46:32)
1997 - J. Vaughters (1:53:54)
1998 - Scott Moninger (1:52:16)
1999 - J. Vaughters (NA)
2000 - Scott Moninger (1:49:42)
2001 - Scott Moninger (1:46:56)
2002 - Scott Moninger (1:50:20)
2003 - J. Vaughters (1:49:29)
2004 - Tom Danielson (1:41:20)*
2005 - Scott Moninger (1:52:50)
2006 - Scott Moninger (1:49:52)

* current record

Mt Washington, New Hampshire:

1997 - Tyler Hamilton (51:56)
1998 - Robert Dapice (59:19)
1999 - Tyler Hamilton (50:21)
2000 - Tim Johnson (55:46)
2001 - Tim Johnson (53:31)
2002 - Tom Danielson (49:24)*
2003 - Tom Danielson (51:05)
2004 - Justin England (58:50)
2005 - Tyler Hamilton (51:11)
2006 - Tyler Hamilton (52:21)

* current record

Additional Climbing Resources

Books:

Cycling Colorado's Mountain Passes by Kurt Magsamen, Fulcrum Publishing, Golden, CO.
Kings of the Mountains by Matt Rendell, Arum Press, London, England.
Uphill Battle by Owen Mulholland, Velopress, Boulder, CO.

Magazines:

Bicycling
Bike Culture
Cycle Sport America
Pro Cycling
Road
Velonews

Selected websites:

Bicyling.com
Cyclingnews.com
Dailypeloton.com
KOMcycling.com
Mountainmapper.com
Northeastcycling.com
Procycling.com
Roadcycling.com
Spokepost.com
Usacycling.org
Velonews.com
Westernwheelers.org

Training:

AthletiCamps.com
Bicyclecoach.com
Bikecamp.com
Carmichael Training Systems (trainright.com)
Coachingbible.com
Cycle-Smart Coaching.com
The Cyclist Training Bible by Joe Friel, Velopress, Boulder, CO.
Eddie B. Cycling World Fitness (Eddiebcyclingworld.com)
EliteFITcoach.com
John Howard Cycling School.com
Peaks Coaching Group.com
Ultrafit.com

Forums:

BikeForums.net
CyclingForums.com
Groups.google.com

KOMcycling.com
Sports.yahoo.com
Tinmtn.org - (Mount Washington Hill Climb Forum)

Touring:

Adventure Cycling Association (aventurecycling.org)
Breaking Away Bicycle Tours (breakingaway.com)
Carpenter/Phinney Bike Camp (bikecamp.com)
Cycle America (cycleamerica.com)
Cycle Tours of Italy (cycleitalia.com)
Timberline Adventures (timbertours.com)
Trek Travel Cycling Vacations (trektravel.com)
Velo Classic Tours (veloclassictours.com)

Events:

Active.com
Azcycling.com
Bikereg.com
Bikeride.com
Cycleidaho.com
Montanacycling.org
Northeastcycling.com
Nmcycling.com
TrueSport.com
Utahcycling.com

A warning of things to come

Climb profiles of the 100 most difficult hill climbs
(in alphabetical order)

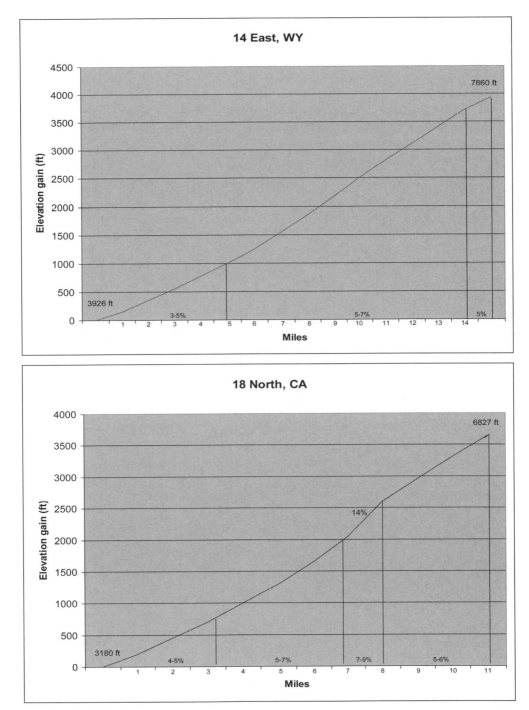

175

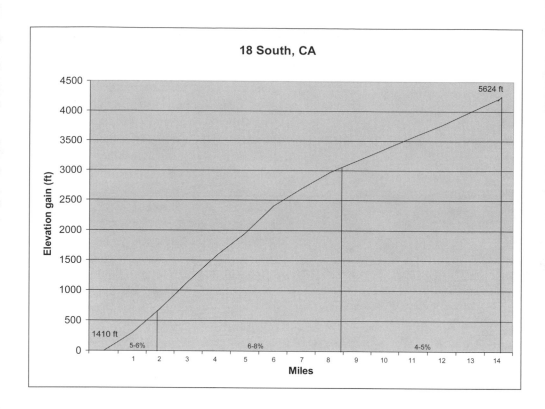

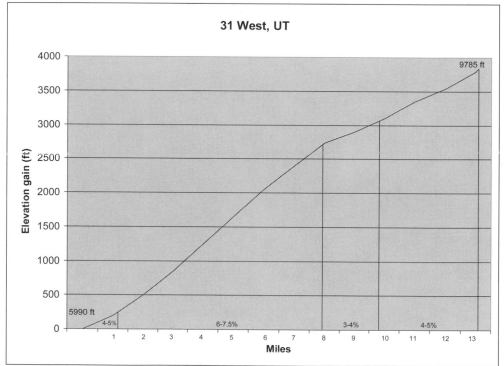

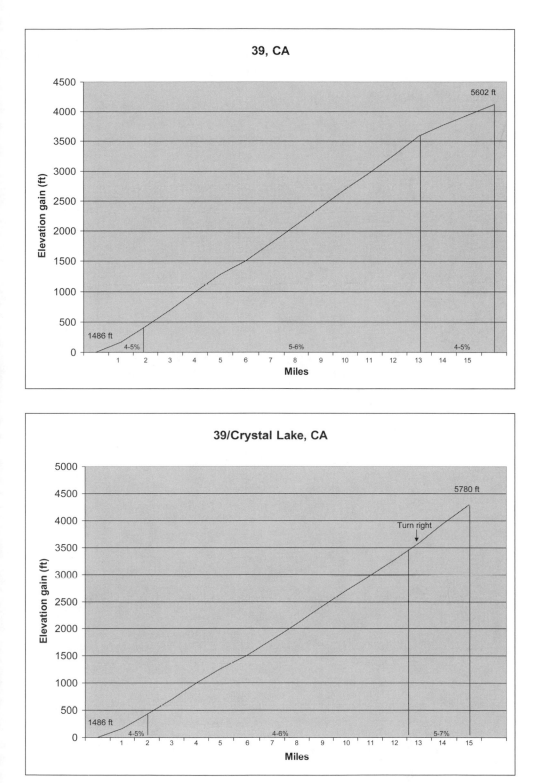

39, CA

39/Crystal Lake, CA

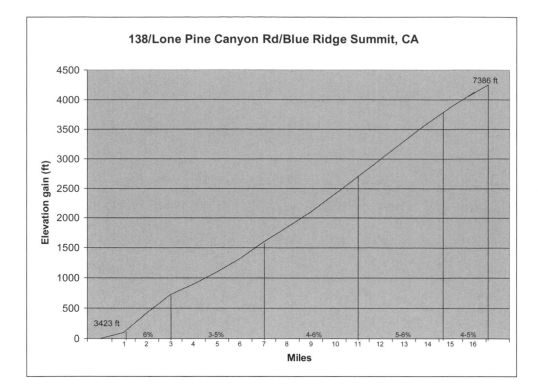

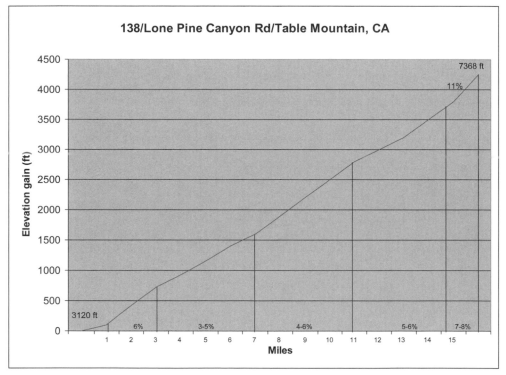

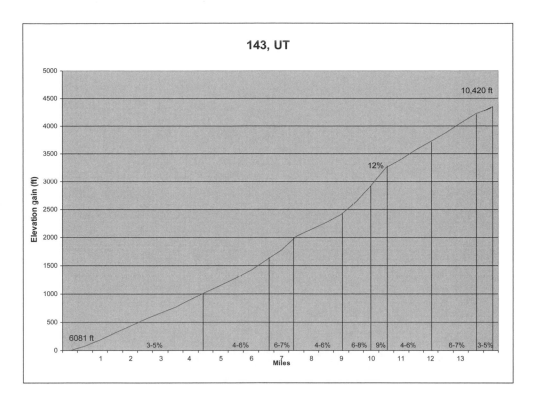

143, UT

Elevation gain (ft)

10,420 ft

12%

6081 ft

3-5% 4-6% 6-7% 4-6% 6-8% 9% 4-6% 6-7% 3-5%

Miles

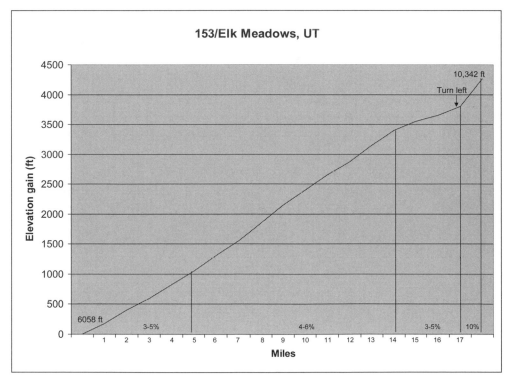

153/Elk Meadows, UT

Elevation gain (ft)

10,342 ft

Turn left

6058 ft

3-5% 4-6% 3-5% 10%

Miles

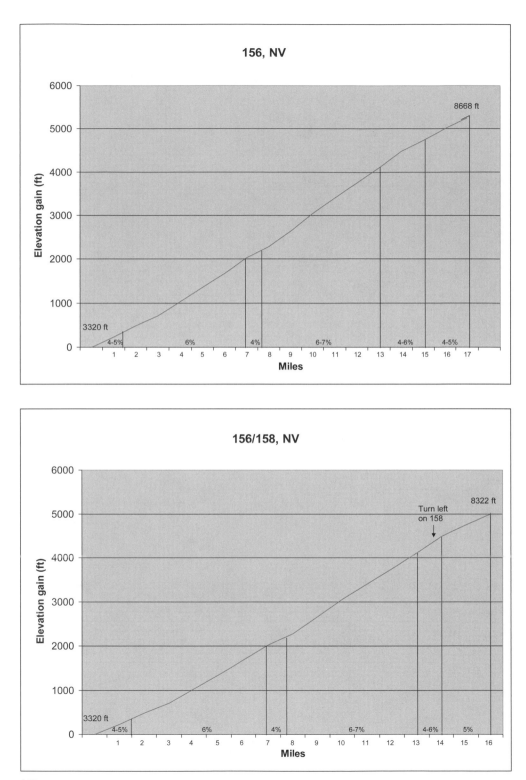

156, NV

156/158, NV

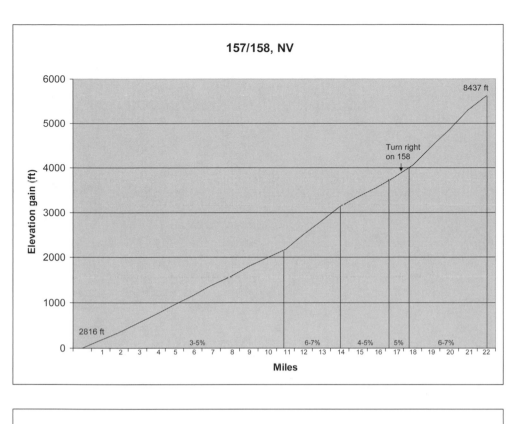

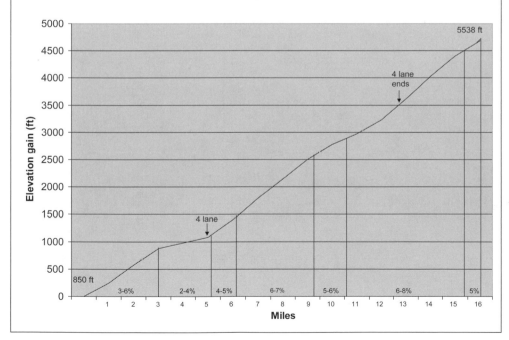

181

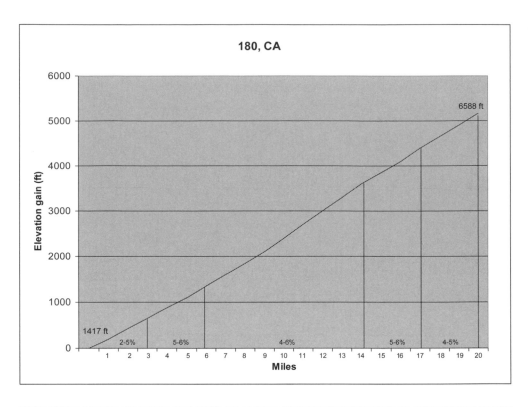

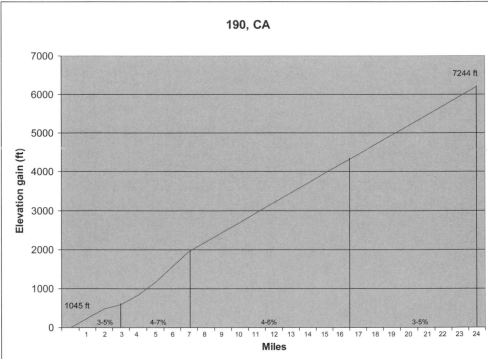

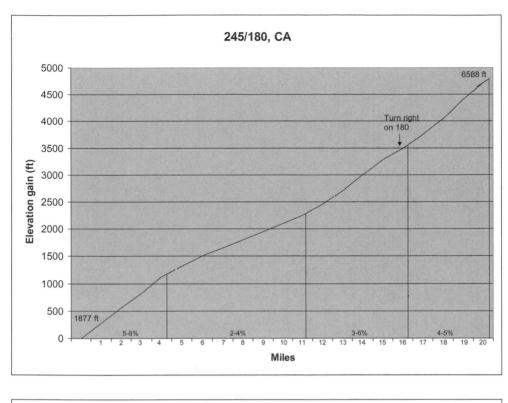

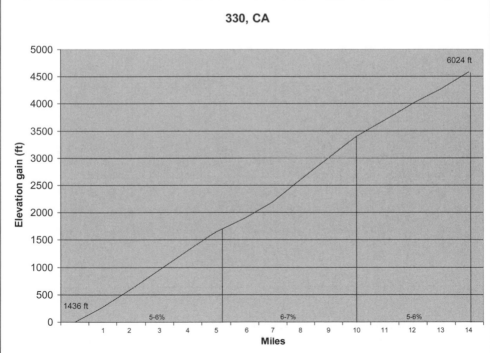

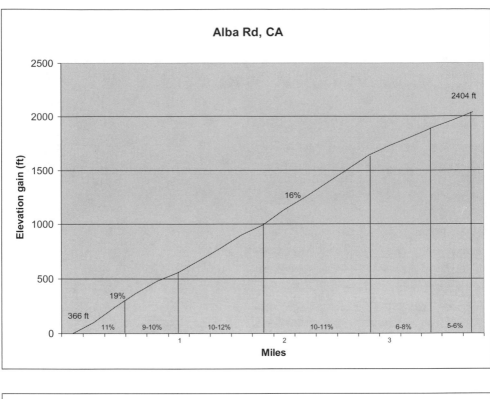

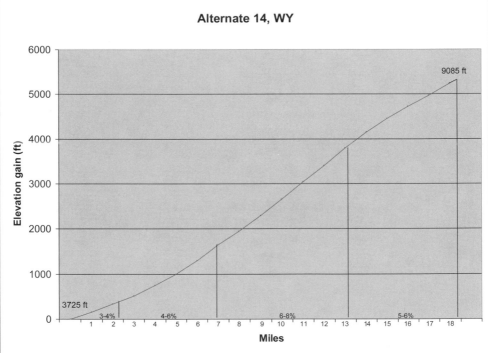

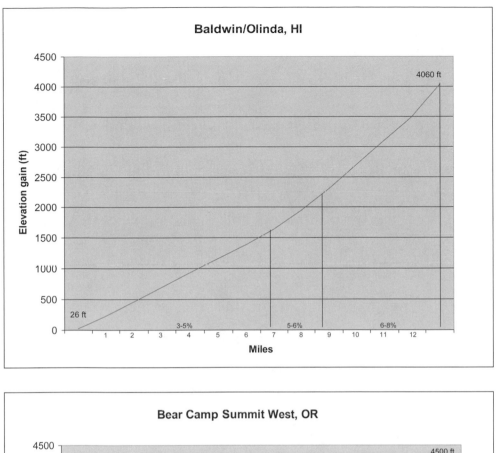

Baldwin/Olinda, HI

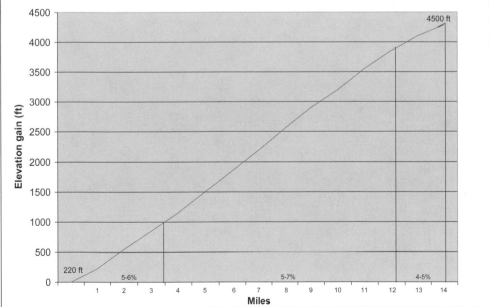

Bear Camp Summit West, OR

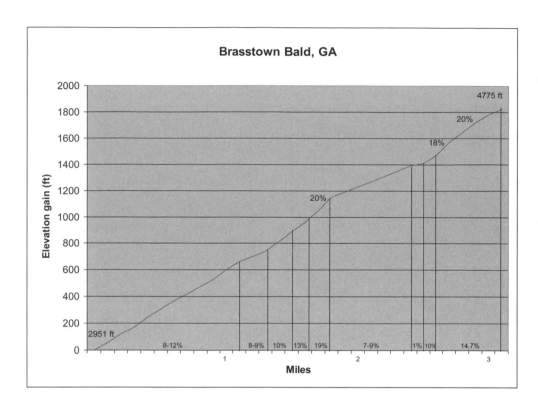

Brasstown Bald, GA

Elevation gain (ft) vs *Miles*

4775 ft
20%
18%
20%
2951 ft
8-12%   8-9% 10% 13% 19%   7-9%   1% 10% 14.7%

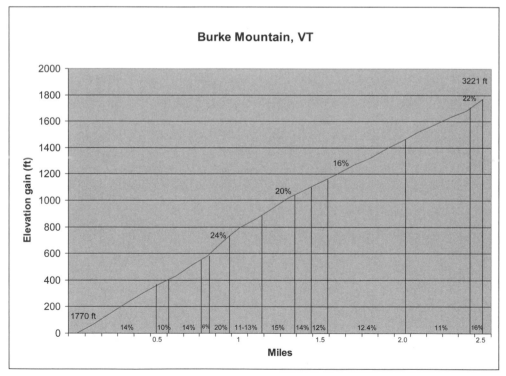

Burke Mountain, VT

Elevation gain (ft) vs *Miles*

3221 ft
22%
16%
20%
24%
1770 ft
14% 10% 14% 6% 20% 11-13% 15% 14% 12%   12.4%   11%   16%

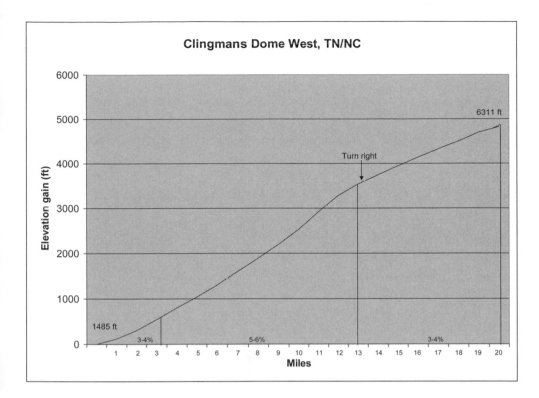

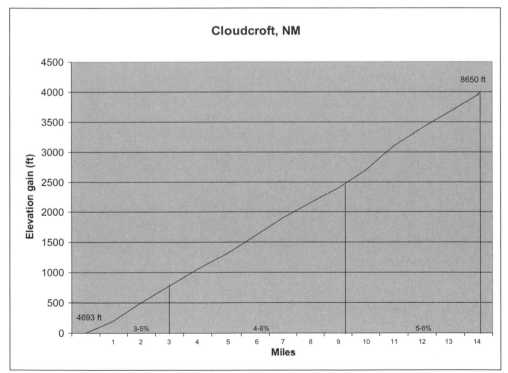

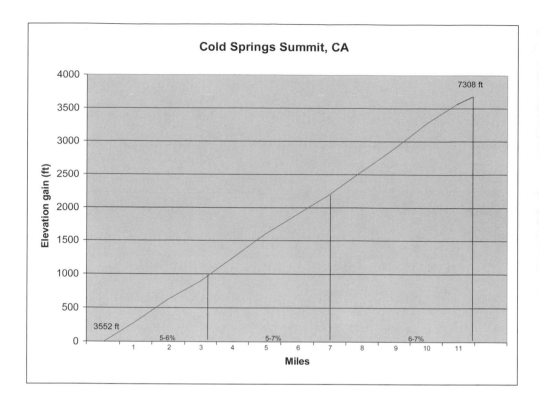

Cold Springs Summit, CA

Elevation gain (ft)

7308 ft

3552 ft

5-6% 5-7% 6-7%

Miles

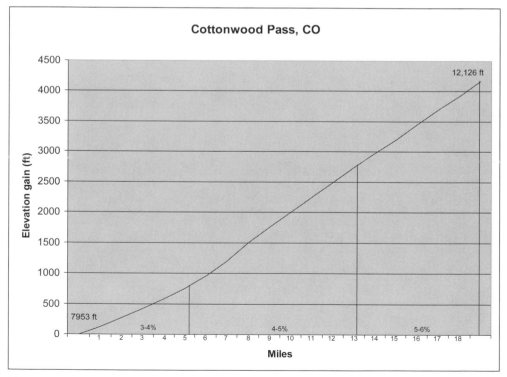

Cottonwood Pass, CO

Elevation gain (ft)

12,126 ft

7953 ft

3-4% 4-5% 5-6%

Miles

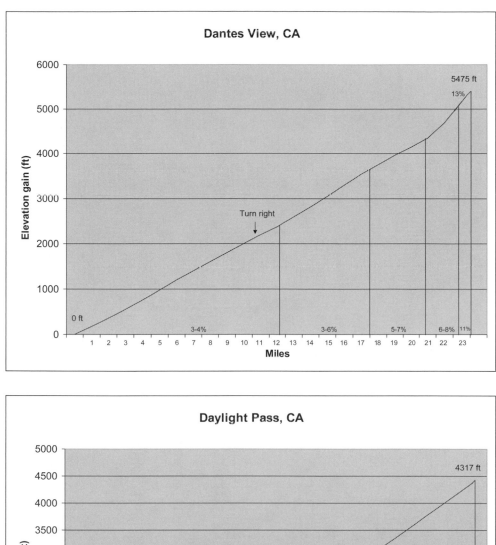

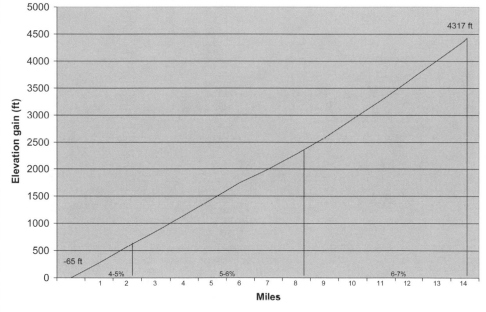

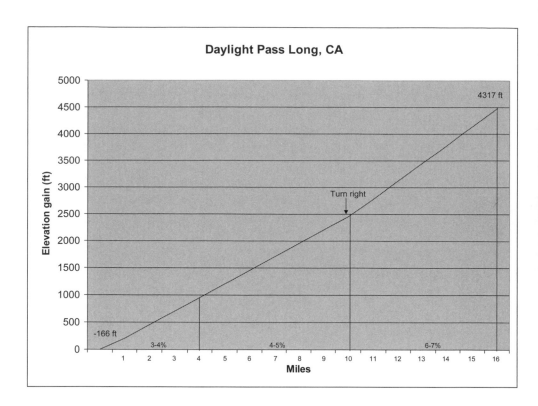

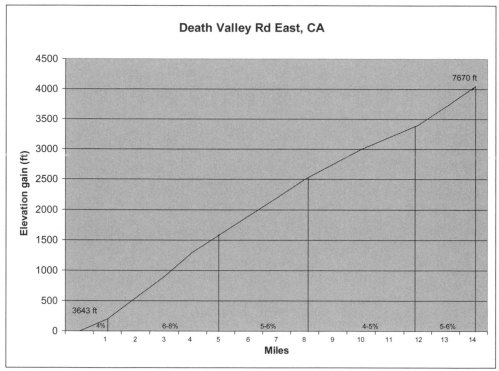

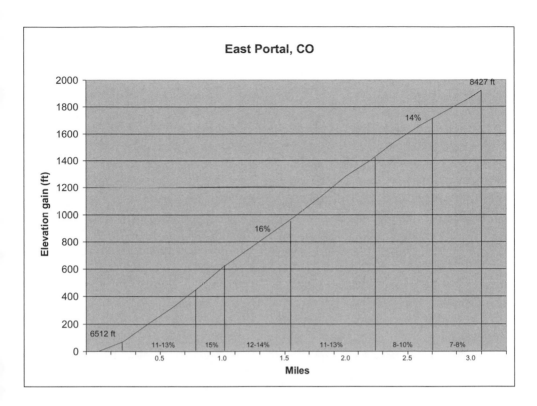

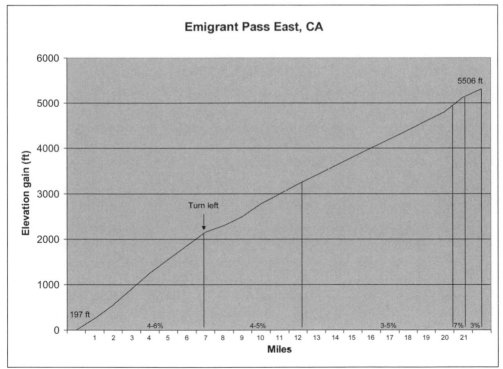

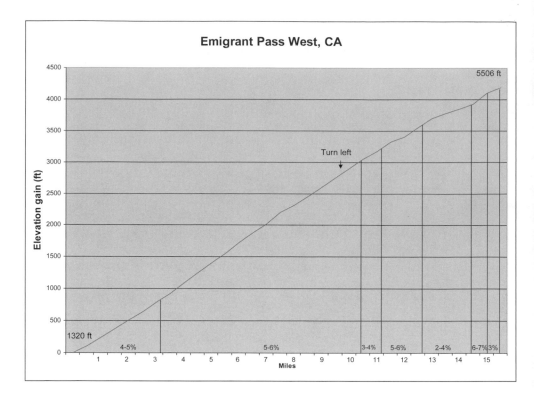

Emigrant Pass West, CA

5506 ft

1320 ft

4-5% 5-6% 3-4% 5-6% 2-4% 6-7% 3%

Turn left

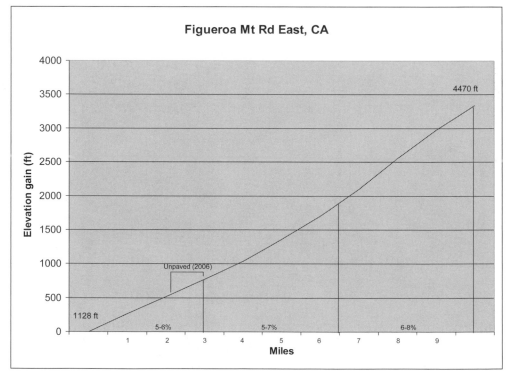

Figueroa Mt Rd East, CA

4470 ft

1128 ft

Unpaved (2006)

5-6% 5-7% 6-8%

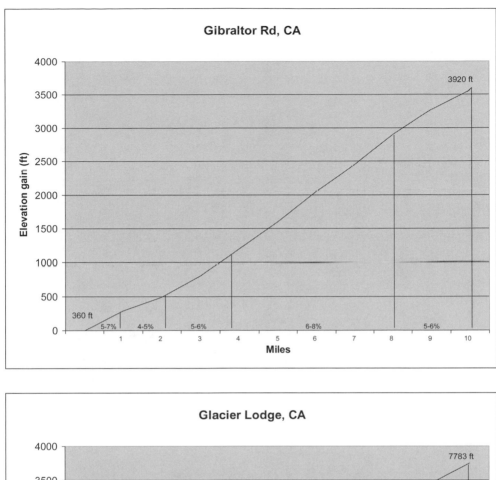

Gibraltor Rd, CA

Elevation gain (ft) vs. Miles

3920 ft

360 ft

5-7% | 4-5% | 5-6% | 6-8% | 5-6%

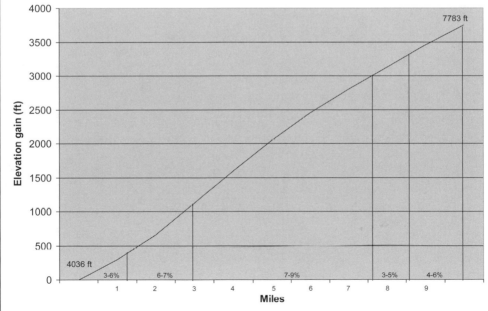

Glacier Lodge, CA

Elevation gain (ft) vs. Miles

7783 ft

4036 ft

3-6% | 6-7% | 7-9% | 3-5% | 4-6%

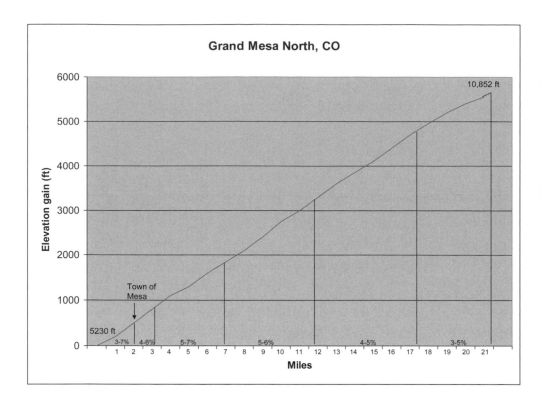

Grand Mesa North, CO

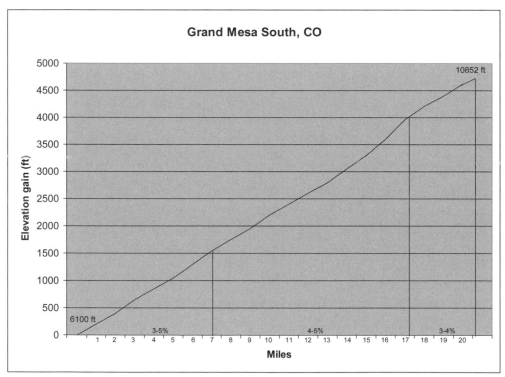

Grand Mesa South, CO

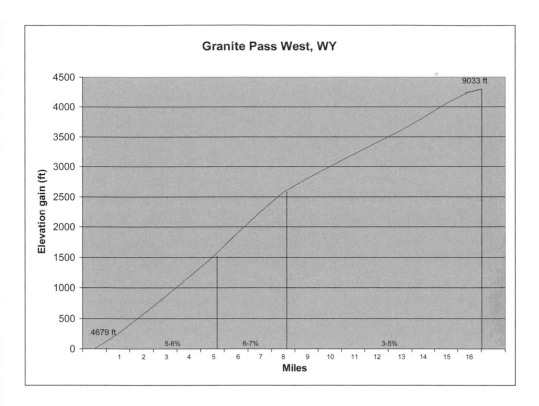

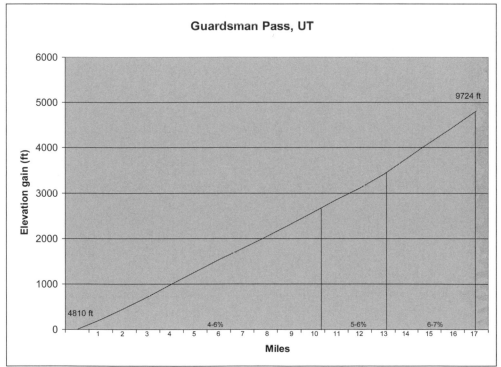

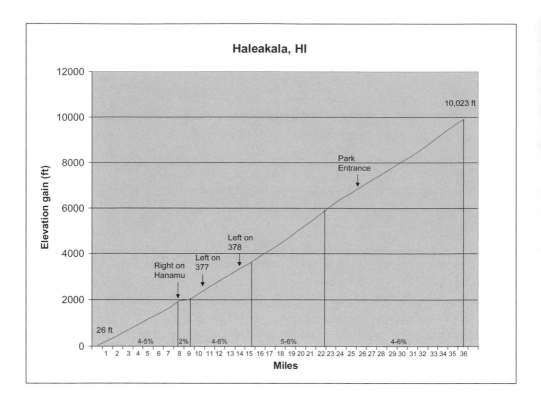

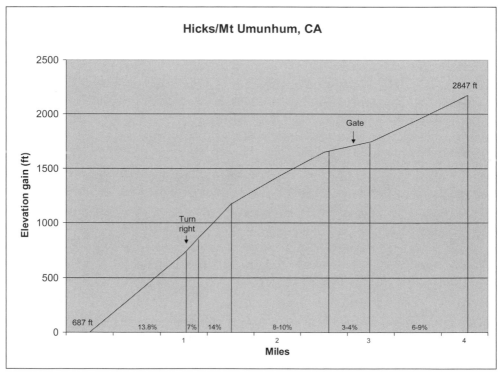

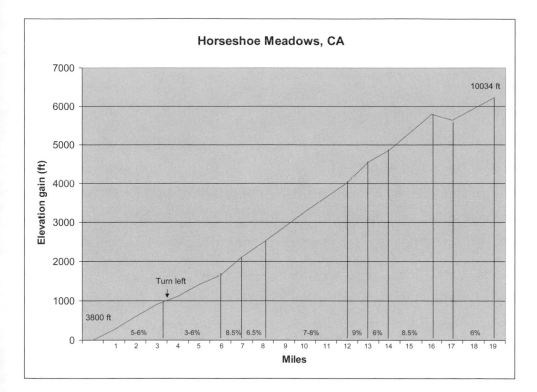

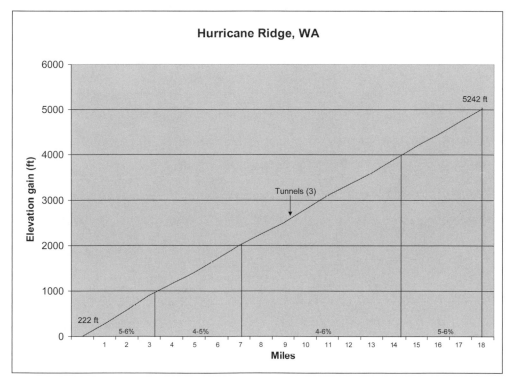

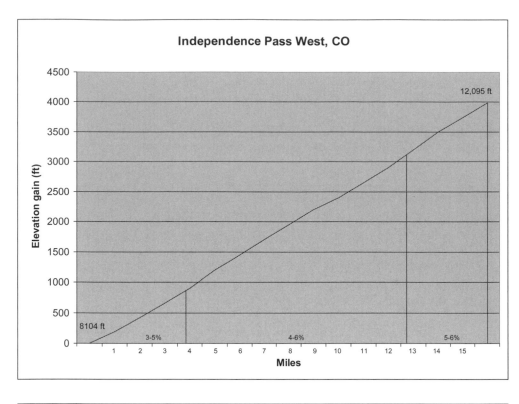

Independence Pass West, CO

Elevation gain (ft) / Miles

12,095 ft

8104 ft

3-5%   4-6%   5-6%

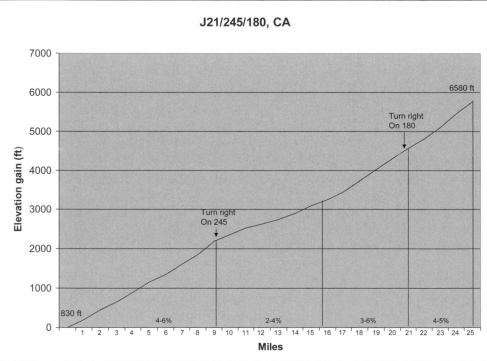

J21/245/180, CA

Elevation gain (ft) / Miles

6580 ft

Turn right
On 180

Turn right
On 245

830 ft

4-6%   2-4%   3-6%   4-5%

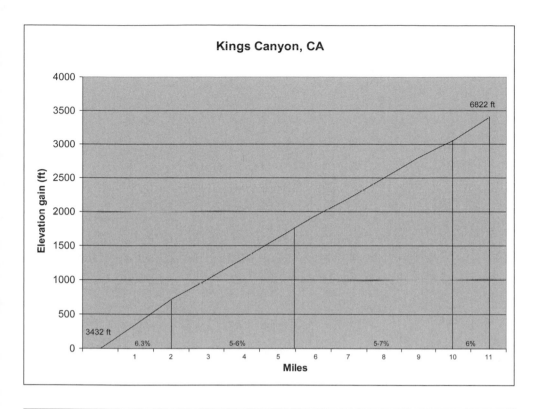

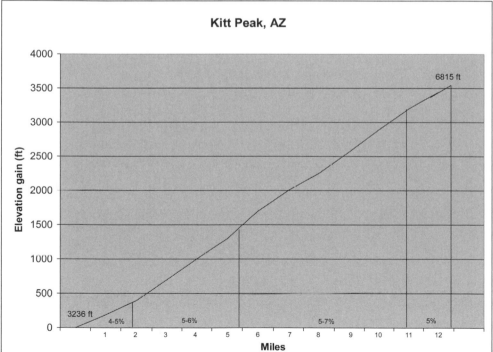

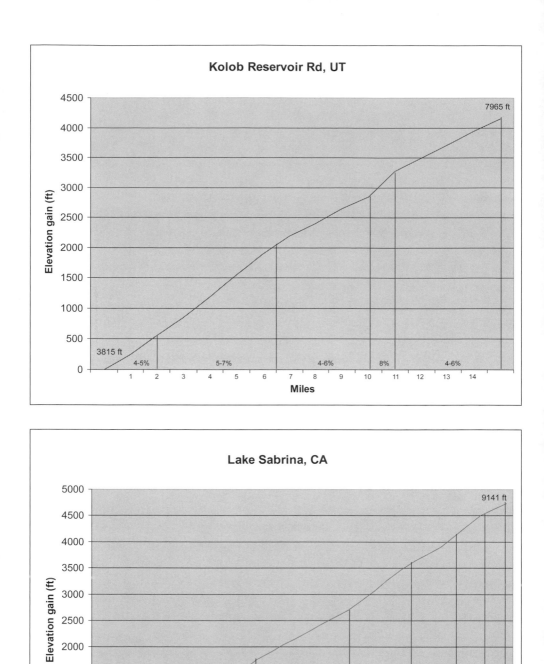

Kolob Reservoir Rd, UT

Elevation gain (ft)

7965 ft

3815 ft

4-5% 5-7% 4-6% 8% 4-6%

Miles

Lake Sabrina, CA

Elevation gain (ft)

9141 ft

4407 ft

3-5% 6-7% 4-6% 6-8% 5-6% 6-8% 4%

Miles

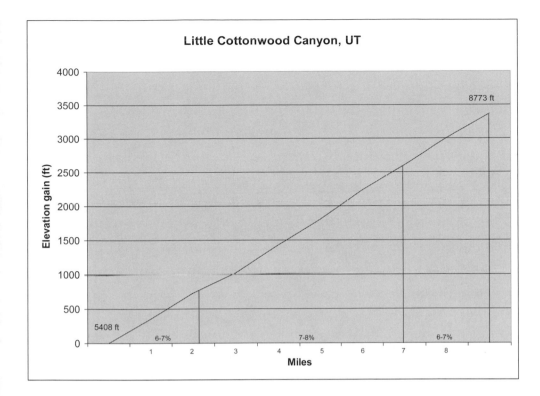

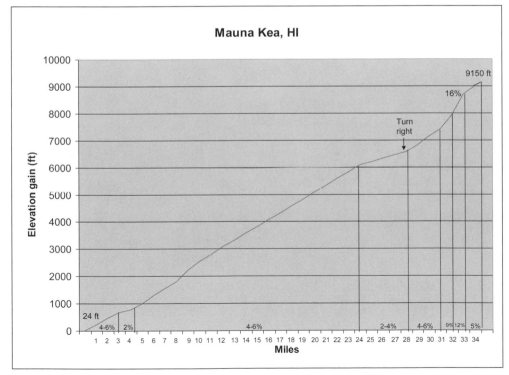

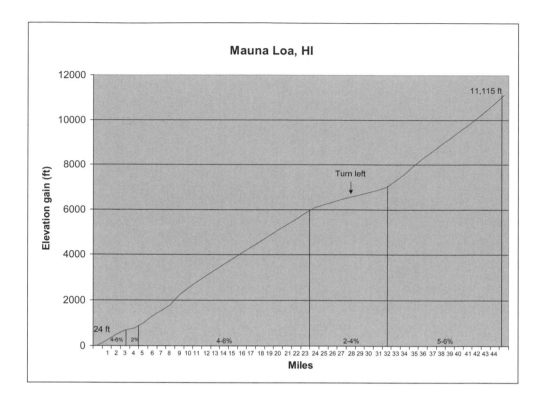

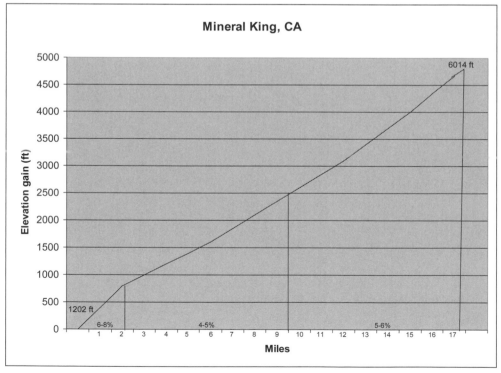

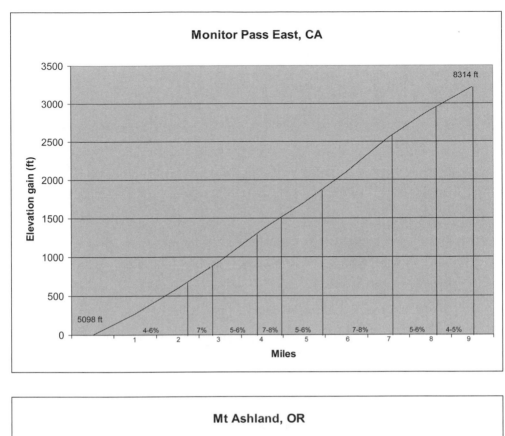

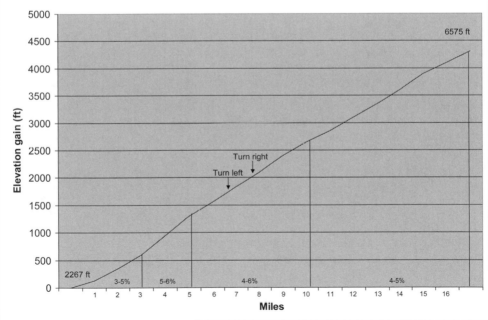

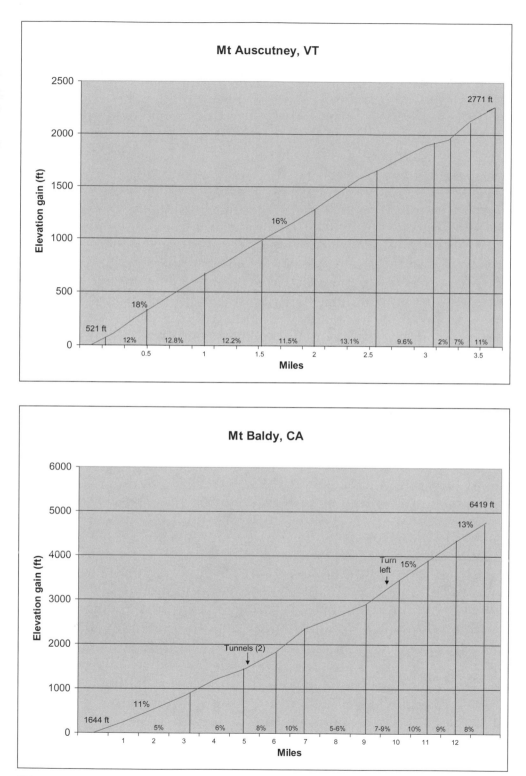

Mt Auscutney, VT

Elevation gain (ft)

2771 ft

16%

18%

521 ft

12%   12.8%   12.2%   11.5%   13.1%   9.6%   2%   7%   11%

Miles

Mt Baldy, CA

Elevation gain (ft)

6419 ft

13%

Turn left   15%

Tunnels (2)

1644 ft

11%

5%   6%   8%   10%   5-6%   7-9%   10%   9%   8%

Miles

204

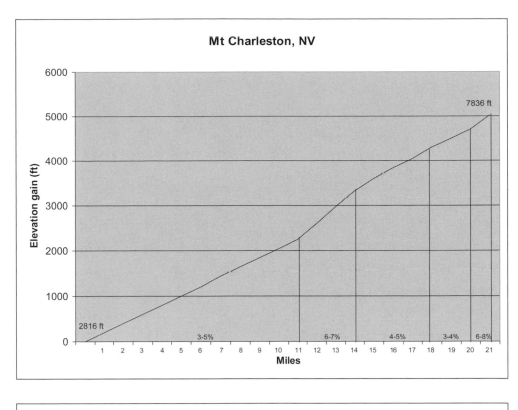

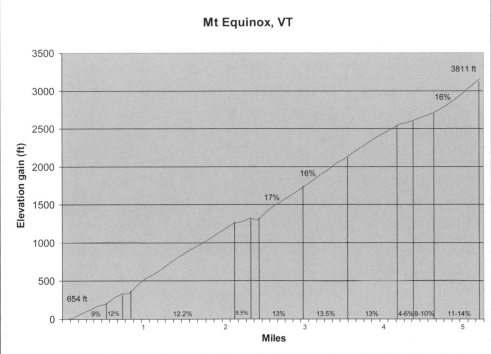

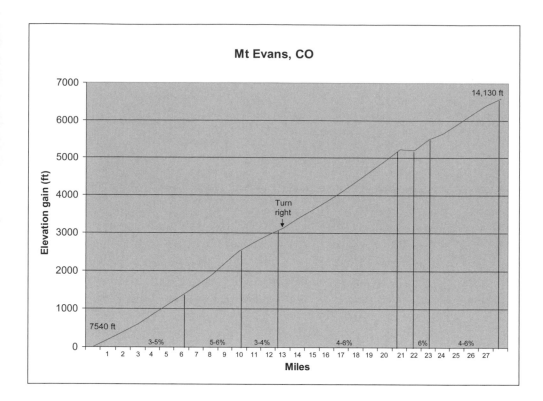

Mt Evans, CO

Elevation gain (ft)

14,130 ft

Turn
right

7540 ft

3-5% 5-6% 3-4% 4-6% 6% 4-6%

Miles

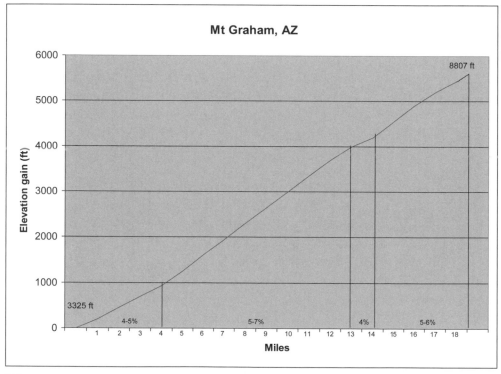

Mt Graham, AZ

Elevation gain (ft)

8807 ft

3325 ft

4-5% 5-7% 4% 5-6%

Miles

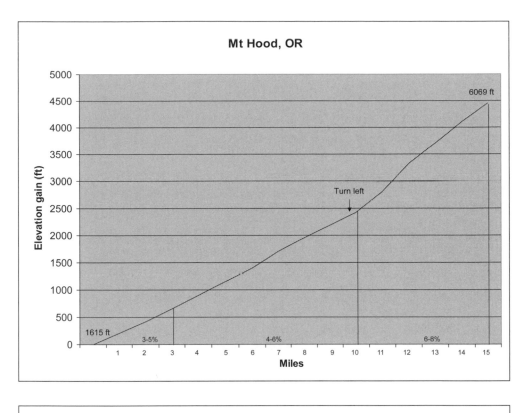

Mt Hood, OR

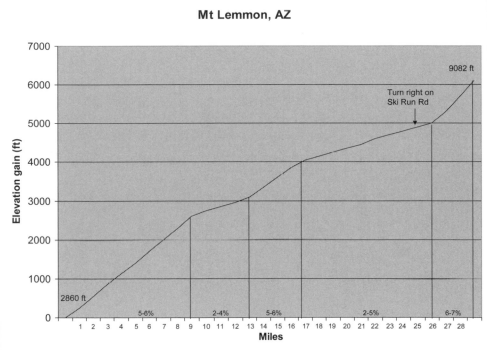

Mt Lemmon, AZ

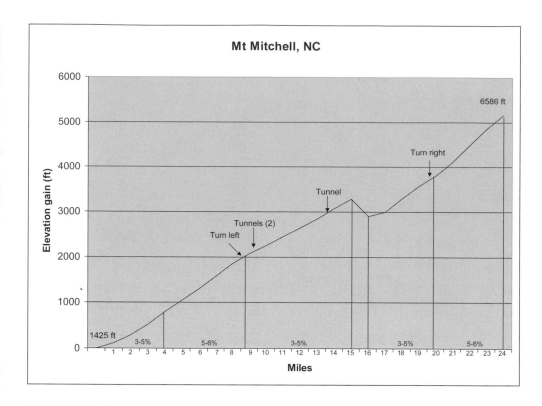

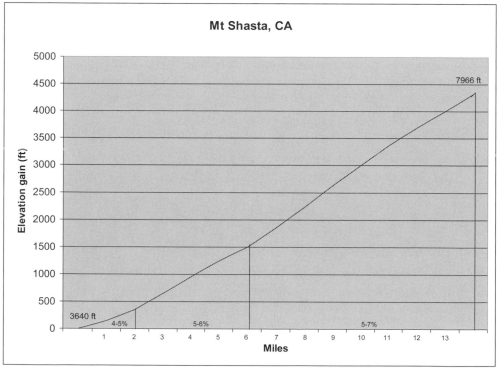

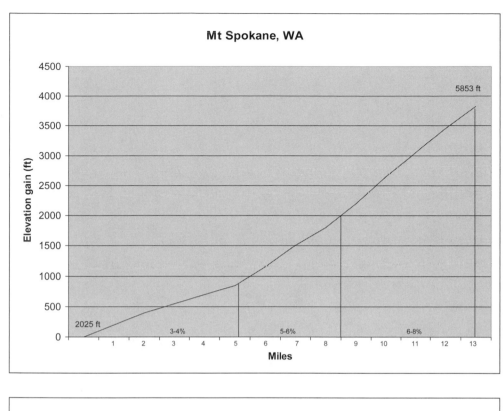

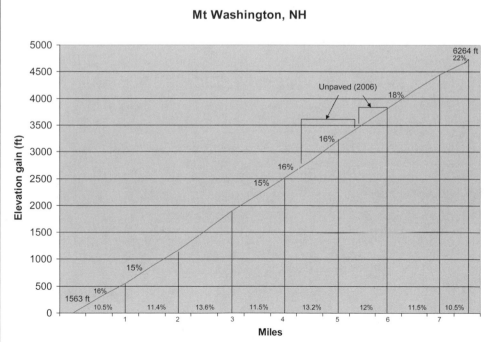

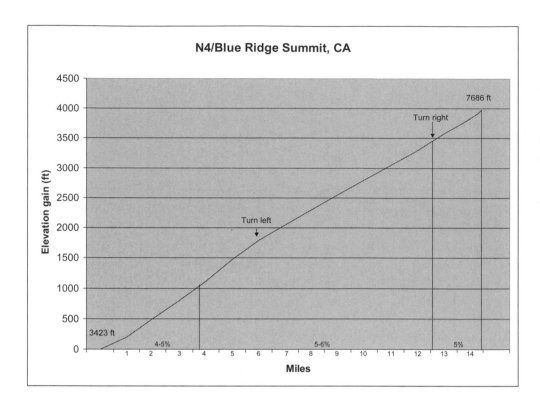

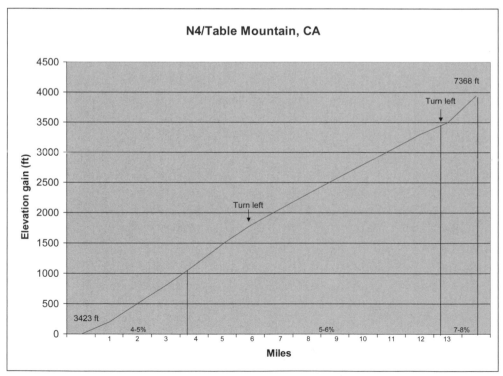

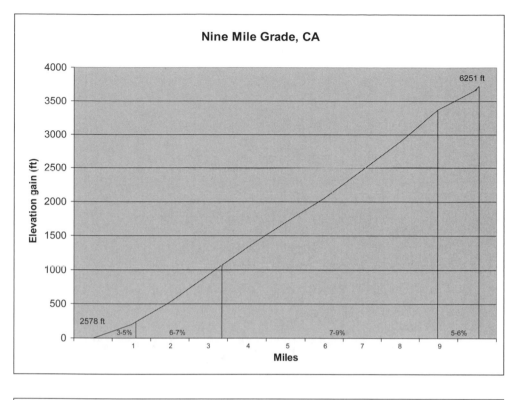

Nine Mile Grade, CA

6251 ft

2578 ft
3-5% 6-7% 7-9% 5-6%

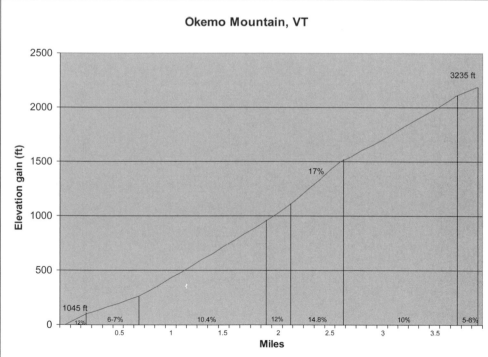

Okemo Mountain, VT

3235 ft

17%

1045 ft
12% 6-7% 10.4% 12% 14.8% 10% 5-6%

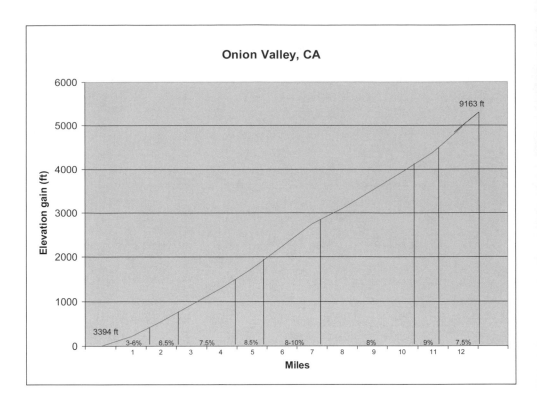

Onion Valley, CA

Elevation gain (ft)

9163 ft

3394 ft

3-6% | 6.5% | 7.5% | 8.5% | 8-10% | 8% | 9% | 7.5%

Miles

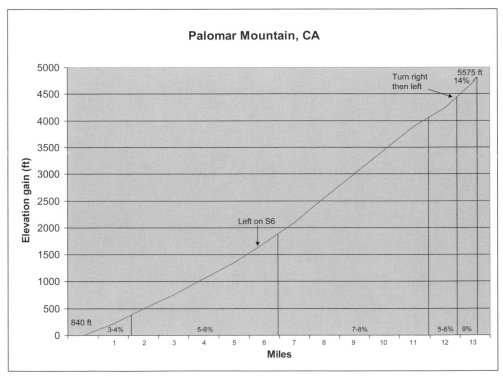

Palomar Mountain, CA

Elevation gain (ft)

Turn right then left

5575 ft
14%

Left on S6

840 ft

3-4% | 5-6% | 7-8% | 5-6% | 9%

Miles

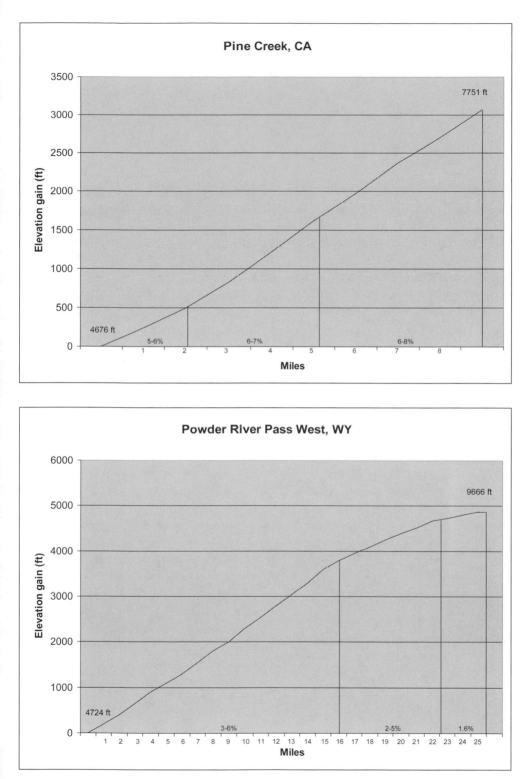

Pine Creek, CA

Elevation gain (ft)

7751 ft

4676 ft

5-6%   6-7%   6-8%

Miles

Powder River Pass West, WY

Elevation gain (ft)

9666 ft

4724 ft

3-6%   2-5%   1.6%

Miles

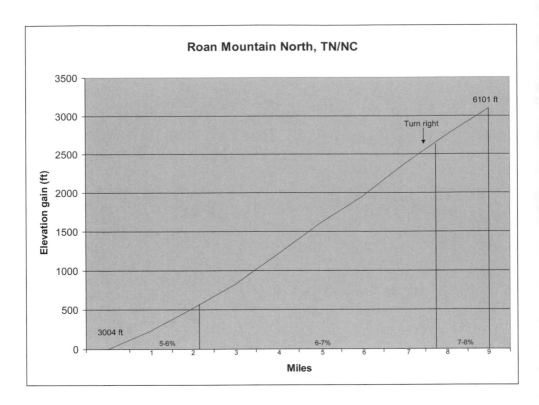

Roan Mountain North, TN/NC

Elevation gain (ft)

6101 ft

Turn right

3004 ft

5-6%   6-7%   7-8%

Miles

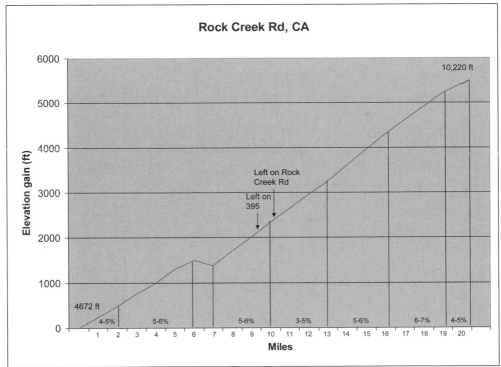

Rock Creek Rd, CA

Elevation gain (ft)

10,220 ft

Left on Rock
Creek Rd

Left on
395

4672 ft

4-5%   5-6%   5-6%   3-5%   5-6%   6-7%   4-5%

Miles

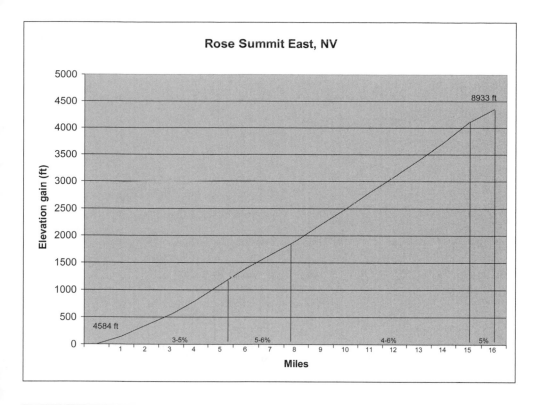

Rose Summit East, NV

Elevation gain (ft)

8933 ft

4584 ft

3-5% 5-6% 4-6% 5%

Miles

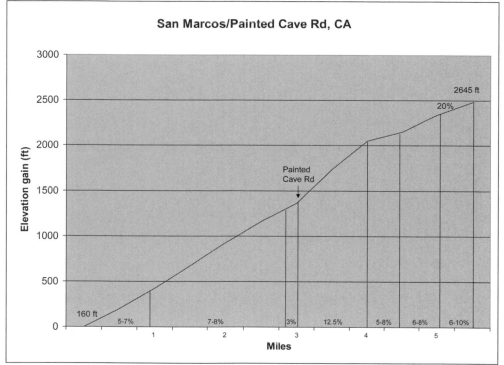

San Marcos/Painted Cave Rd, CA

Elevation gain (ft)

2645 ft

20%

Painted
Cave Rd

160 ft

5-7% 7-8% 3% 12.5% 5-8% 6-8% 6-10%

Miles

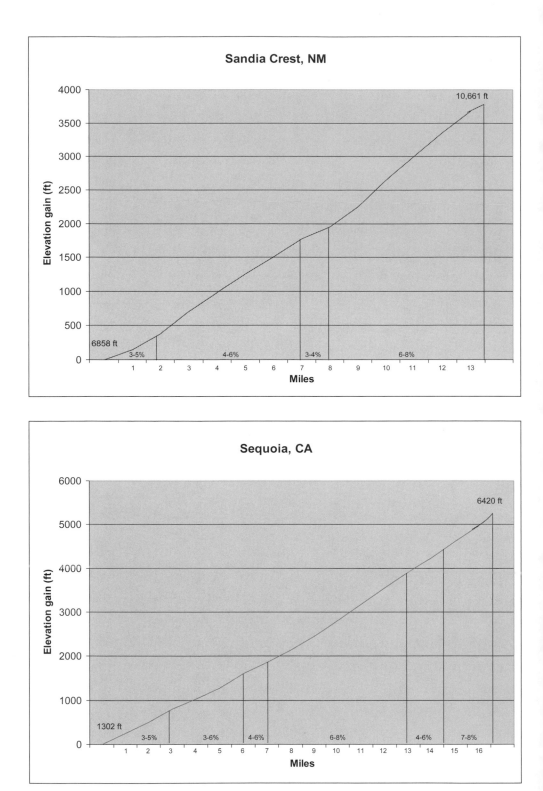

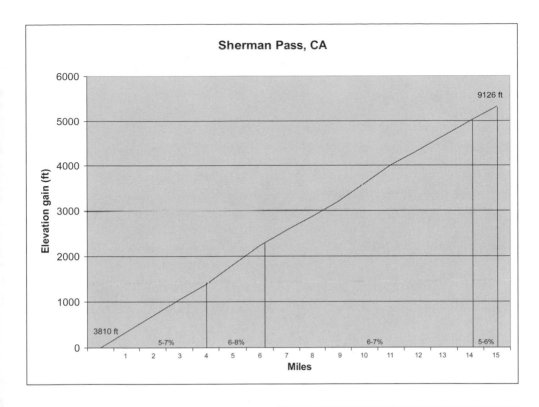

Sherman Pass, CA

Elevation gain (ft)

9126 ft

3810 ft

5-7%   6-8%   6-7%   5-6%

Miles

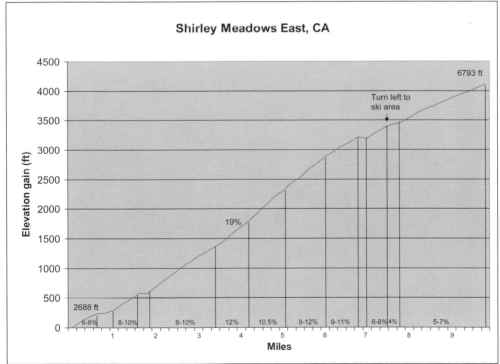

Shirley Meadows East, CA

Elevation gain (ft)

6793 ft

Turn left to ski area

19%

2688 ft

6-8%   8-10%   8-10%   12%   10.5%   8-12%   9-11%   6-8% 4%   5-7%

Miles

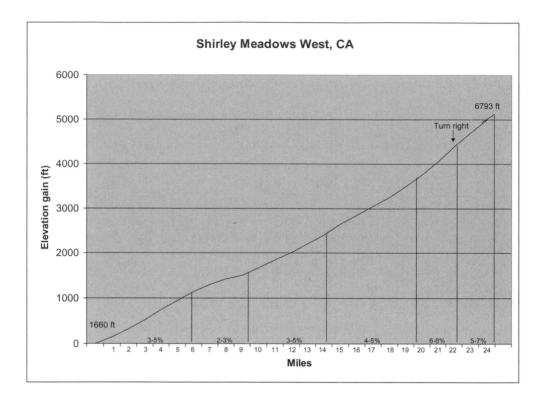

Shirley Meadows West, CA

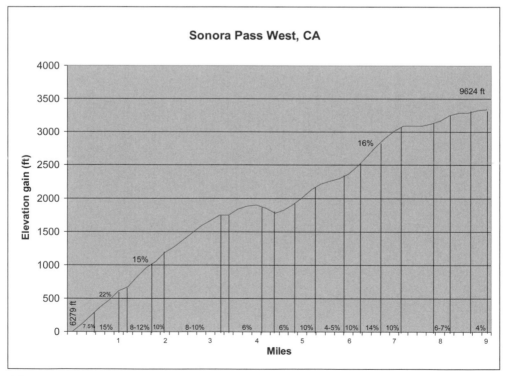

Sonora Pass West, CA

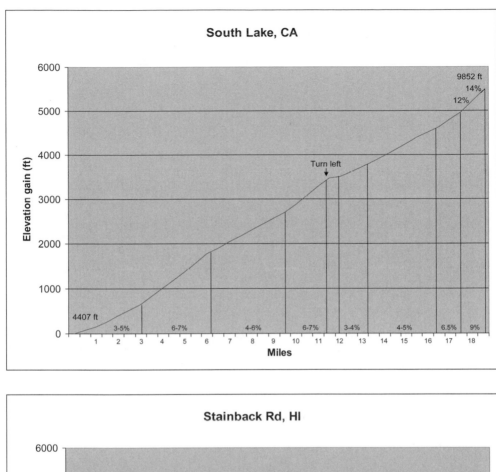

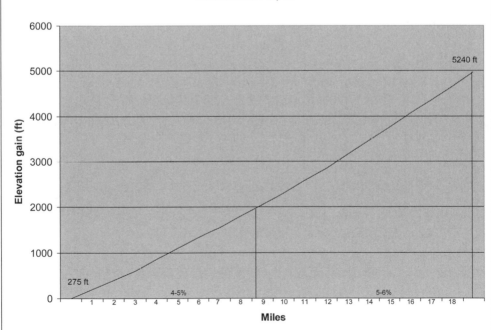

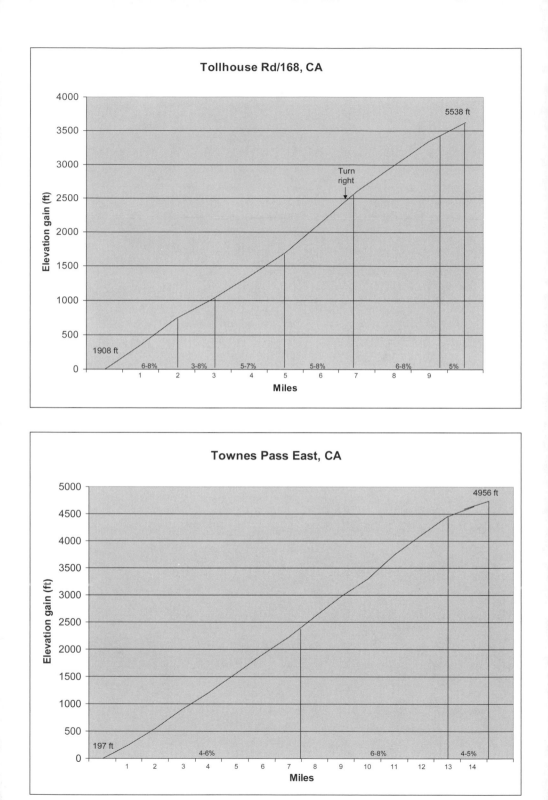

Tollhouse Rd/168, CA

Elevation gain (ft)

5538 ft

Turn right

1908 ft

6-8% 3-8% 5-7% 5-8% 6-8% 5%

Miles

Townes Pass East, CA

Elevation gain (ft)

4956 ft

197 ft

4-6% 6-8% 4-5%

Miles

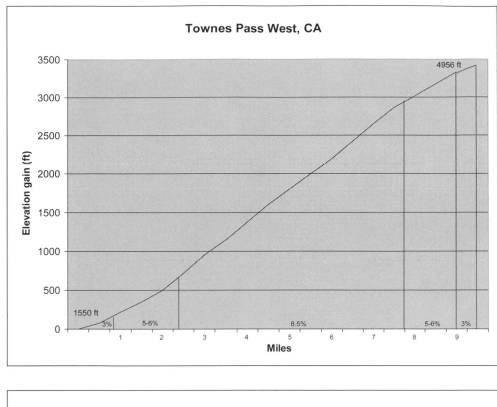

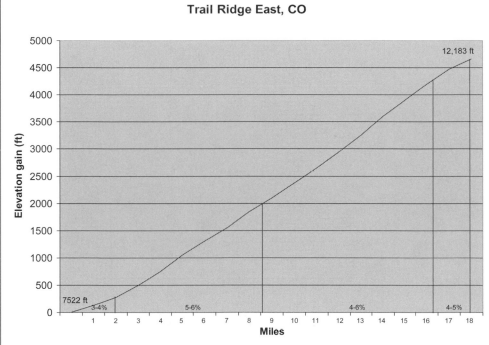

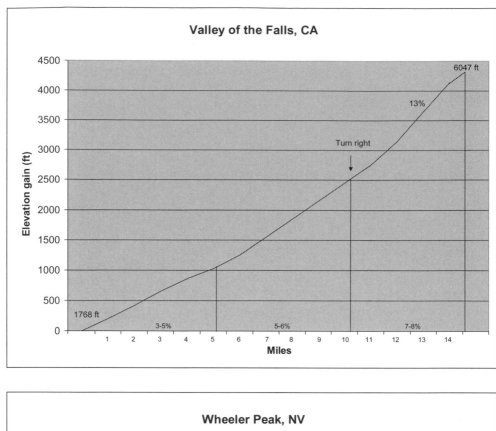

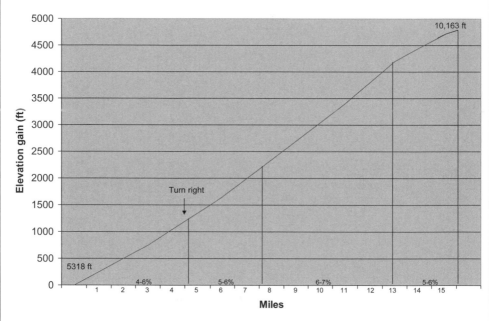